Books by DEBORAH TALL

The Island of the White Cow: Memories of an Irish Island
1986
Ninth Life (poetry)
1982
Eight Colors Wide (poetry)
1974

The Island of the White Cow

THE ISLAND
OF THE
WHITE COW

Memories of an Irish Island

DEBORAH TALL

ATHENEUM   *New York* 1987

Deborah Tall's poem "Crossing" was published in
Ninth Life, a collection of her poetry (Ithaca House, 1982),
and is used by permission of the publisher.

The extracts from *Islands and Authors* by Proinsias
O'Conluain, and from *Letters from the Great Blasket* by
Eibhlís Ní Shúilleabháin, are used by permission of the
publishers, The Mercier Press Ltd., Cork.

The lines from the poem "The Great Hunger" by
Patrick Kavanagh are used by permission of the publisher,
Devin-Adair Publishers, Greenwich, Connecticut.

*Atheneum
Macmillan Publishing Company
866 Third Avenue, New York, N.Y. 10022
Collier Macmillan Canada, Inc.*

*Library of Congress Cataloging in Publication Data
Tall, Deborah, 1951–
The Island of the White Cow.
1. Tall, Deborah, 1951–   —Homes and haunts—Ireland—Connemara.
2. Connemara (Ireland)—Description and travel.   3. Islands—Ireland.
4. Poets, American—20th century—Biography.   I. Title.
PS3570.A397Z477   1986   811'.54' [B]   85-47643
ISBN 0-689-11650-0 (hard cover)
ISBN 0-689-70722-3 (paperback)*

*Macmillan books are available at special discounts for bulk purchases
for sales promotions, premiums, fund-raising, or educational use.
For details, contact:*

*Special Sales Director
Macmillan Publishing Company
866 Third Avenue
New York, N.Y. 10022*

*First American paperback edition
2 4 6 8 10 9 7 5 3 1
Printed in the United States of America*

For the islanders
with the hope that you will always be islanders

and for my family

*Whatever happens on this Island I have one
gifted thing to tell you of it I was always
happy there. I was happy among sorrows on
this Island. I think I will not be interesting in
life atall from this on when I am gone out on
the Mainland.*

> —Eibhlís Ní Shúilleabháin,
> *Letters from the Great Blasket*

Preface

 Though the division of the book into four seasons suggests it takes place over a single year, the span between the events of the first spring and the last winter is, in fact, five years. Poetic license aside, time as we know it has but a shaky hold on enchanted islands.

I'm indebted to many of the wonderful books that have been written about Irish islands: Peig Sayers's autobiography, *Peig;* Maurice O'Sullivan's *Twenty Years A-Growing;* Eibhlís Ní Shúilleabháin's *Letters from the Great Blasket;* Tomás O'Crohan's *The Islandman;* Pat Mullen's *Man of Aran;* J. M. Synge's *The Aran Islands;* Robin Flower's *The Western Island;* Heinrich Böll's *Irish Journal;* Kenneth McNally's *The Islands of Ireland;* and Proinsias O'Conluain's anthology of essays, *Islands and Authors.*

The many details concerning Grania Uaile are from Anne Chambers's biography, *Graniauaile: The Life and Times of Grace O'Malley.* The legend about islands and whales is recounted from T. H. White's *The Bestiary.* I've also been helped by Seán MacGiollarnáth's

Conamara; The Clare Island Survey of 1915; the poetry of Patrick Kavanagh; and an article dated 1921, found in typescript, written by the Rev. John Neary.

Additionally, I'm grateful to Yaddo for residencies during which much of the book was written, and to many generous friends for their helpful readings of the manuscript.

Finally, I've been educated and inspired by the islanders, and by a man here called Owen. To them, my ultimate gratitude.

The First Spring

> *Somewhere among the note-books of Gideon I once found a list of diseases as yet unclassified by medical science, and among these there occurred the word* Islomania, *which was described as a rare but by no means unknown affliction of spirit. There are people, Gideon used to say, by way of explanation, who find islands somehow irresistible. The mere knowledge that they are on an island, a little world surrounded by the sea, fills them with an indescribable intoxication.*
>
> —Lawrence Durrell,
> *Reflections on a Marine Venus*

Beside me, a suitcase full of broken dishes hauled halfway around the world: an emblem of trepidation—the only I've allowed myself. At this far edge of civilization, I'd intended, as a single luxury and link to the past, to eat off my grandmother's cornflower-blue plates; but that small pleasure is not to be mine.

I am going to an island off the west coast of Ireland with an Irish writer. The thought still jolts me.

Owen and I met last fall during my last year of college, he a visiting writer in the English Department, twenty years my senior. It is hard now to describe the impact of meeting him, the power of his presence in a room, the shock, later, of his attraction to me. I was struck at once by his vigor, by his flowing, bright white hair and dazzling sea-blue eyes set in a slim, handsome face. His voice was mellifluous, sirenic. Listening to him in class was more like watching a one-man show, the script of which got written on the spot. Despite his age, he had more vitality than most of us did, and certainly more than any other professor I'd come across. He was a revelation, live fire sweeping through the deadwood of a Midwestern American campus, blasting conventional pieties and scorning mediocrities. His purism, enthusiasm, and unconventionality ignited us, made devotees and idealists of the entire class—especially the girls.

When I asked him once, on behalf of several friends, if he'd come talk about Yeats some evening at our dorm, he said no, but that he'd talk to *me* about Yeats one evening over a drink. I froze. If he'd said over a cup of coffee, or a joint, maybe I'd have agreed and lied to the other girls. I'd never been to a bar in my life. Owen and I needed a translator.

But when he returned my first paper for the course bannered with "Stunningly good" and demanded in a note that I come to see him in his office to talk about it and "multifarious other related and unrelated matters," I did.

We were soon having dinners in off-campus hideaways where he pontificated, recited, sang, and advised how I, an aspirant poet, ought to proceed with my life: "The writer must live like a vagabond, at the edge of society, like the early Irish bard who earned his way by his songs, camping on the doorsteps of those that denied him. God help those that *did!*" He made it sound obvious, inevitable.

Is that how he lived? It's how he was trying to live. He'd escaped to an island before with his family in tow. It was an Irish-speaking island and he'd perfected his grasp of the language while embracing the rustic life. It was harsh, wildly stormy, and his wife's nerve broke; she shepherded the children back to Dublin and Owen soon followed, resentful. Now he meant to find another island and stay. He'd left his wife and children and was going off to the West of Ireland after this teaching stint. Wasn't he afraid? "Fear, child, has no place in the life

4

of the artist." Was it fair to exact that price from his family? "There's no fairness in the world," he said.

And he crooned me poetry. "Ah, penny, brown penny, brown penny,/I am looped in the loops of her hair. . . ." And I listened and got looped in the loops of his voice. His enthusiasm was infectious, subversive. Before long, he had talked me out of graduate school and onto a plane to the West of Ireland with tales of the enchanted landscape and the kind of simple, communal life I so obviously needed to experience, he said, after a sheltered, upper-middle-class, secularized upbringing in an arid suburb of Philadelphia, the daughter of first-generation Americans of Eastern European Jewish background risen from poverty to affluence. I knew I was being talked into something, but I liked what he was talking. I was bored with my life, starved by my surround. I was ready for departure, for adventure, for the discovery of that Europe I felt more drawn to and culturally part of than the country I'd grown up in. It was 1972 and nothing I'd come to believe in had any reality in the world outside the university. There was no place in American society I could imagine leading my life. So I was ready to try what I'd never imagined. I was more than ready. "Ah, penny, brown penny, brown penny,/ One cannot begin it too soon."

These are explanations, but the truth is I was bewitched and my reasoning was vague. A beautiful man was in love with me and he wanted to steal me away and help me realize my dream of being a writer. No matter how my friends stared in amazement, no matter how much pain and outrage it caused my family, I knew I had to go. Owen already knew me—the me I wanted to become—better than people who'd known me for years. He made me believe in the writing of poetry as my calling.

Owen's dedication to the writing life is so great

he will sacrifice almost everything for circumstances conducive to his work. He has inspired me to do likewise, to commit myself, to trust my meagerly evidenced talent and give up material comforts for the sake of having adequate solitude and time to write. On an island we'll be able to live cheaply enough so that little time need be spent pursuing money, at a remove from the commercial world amidst a lively, articulate culture largely untouched by modernity. Can I endure what his first family didn't? Will the kind of stimulation that's good for him be good for me? I'm gambling that this foreign island will, incongruously, allow me for the first time to feel at home in the world.

We are waiting for the boat in Clochan, the island's link to mainland Ireland, in the thick of a spring gale, a blustering April downpour; but we're assured a boat will come. When? There's no saying. It depends on a variety of circumstances: Supply. Demand. The tide. The wind. The skipper's whim. "But doesn't the mail boat make a regular run at noon?" I ask the Clochan bartender. That's what the cardboard sign behind the bar says. He looks at me, impatient but amused: "She'll be here when she gets here."

There's nowhere to wait for the boat under cover of roof in Clochan except under the roof of the Clochan pub. Clochan is a grocery, a butcher, a pub, a pier, and a small parking lot for cars that have been abandoned in favor of the island. Clochan is a place, indeed, largely in existence for the sake of the island, and its residents' faces are bitterly etched with that sad fact. The people of Clochan despise the tourists who are in their village only on sufferance, though tourists provide the only money made in the place: hours of drinking in wait of the island boat. The name of the townland where the boat ties up is Irish, Owen tells me, for "The Skull."

A local with decades of grievance in his voice and weeks of grime on his face tells me to drink brandy if I'm afraid of getting seasick. "It won't be a calm crossing . . . if she comes at all," he warns churlishly. Two brandies later, no sign of the boat, I try to get coffee, but it's not to be had.

To sober, I stand on Clochan pier, face into the gale, straining to find the island on the plate of grey, spattered sea. Only the dark thrust of the haphazard coastline and a few offshore deposits of uninhabitable rock break the monotony. Half a dozen fishing boats tied to the concrete pier rock nonchalantly with all the time in the world.

At this far end of Connemara, even the dull, angry grey of the water comes like a blessing. The remote, wild, but undeniably beguiling stretch of Connemara we've journeyed through to get here is as terrifying as it is beautiful. It is a landscape that, despite the remarkable drama of its swiftly changing light and shifting skyline, is nothing so much as stoic. The airy blue of the mountains is untillable rock from which not a tree grows, not even at sea level in the rubble of glacial waste where only gorse tenaciously clings; the spongy bog that buckles the road into a roller coaster sinks into itself indifferently until it hits rock; and other than rock and bog there is nothing but a great open space of wind and color. As Cromwell said of nearby County Clare: not enough water to drown a man, not enough of a tree to hang a man, not enough earth to bury a man. The only advantage of the scene before me is that there is plenty of water for drowning. Yet there is something intoxicating in this air that's already converting me to a new measure of beauty.

The boat finally arrives—a well-kept blue trawler, sixty or seventy feet long, a graceful scooped bowl atop the water. After all the anticipation, we must wait two more hours till she's ready to leave: there's mail to get, boxes of groceries, newspapers, half a deck-load of concrete blocks slowly unpiled from the pier and repiled on deck. We wait anxiously while the boat heaves in skittish water.

The skipper and his mate ignore us during all this, but later are irritated by the extent of our luggage, and say we should have warned them before they loaded the blocks. Don't we know anything about boats? Who are we, and are we planning to stay a year with all this stuff or what? Jamesy O'Halloran, the gangly mate, hurls himself into the hold and Jack Coyne, gruff skipper and owner, hands down our cases. Both move woodenly, encased in gleaming orange oilskin suits and black wellingtons.

We're directed by a mumble and a twitch of the head to sit on top of the tarpaulin-covered hatch on the open deck as, at last, Jack gracefully maneuvers the boat out from Clochan quay. Once clear, he sits at the rudder blandly staring into the mist and rain out ahead where the island is. Jamesy stands in the bow, biding his time while the diesel engine does what sails and human hands used to. We are the only passengers. No one speaks.

At the head of Clochan Bay, we leave sheltered water and hit the swift channel of water between mainland and island. The boat leaps and twists in a blanket of rain and seawater. The brandy sloshes sickeningly in my stomach and I shiver at each blast of the penetrating wind. Jack's still and calm. He doesn't seem to concentrate on the play of the water, yet he makes crucial adjustments of the rudder just in time for us to glide over oncoming swells. Immediately, I admire this aloof master. Only once do we take water—a wave sweeping the deck like a slap in the face—and he nods apologetically as we shake out. No sign of that fabled, godforsaken bit of rock they call the Island of the White Cow till, fifteen or twenty minutes into the channel, she reveals herself: first her back and one rugged shoulder, and then, at leisure, her full length, more monumental than I had imagined, four miles of rock looming on the horizon. Wiping water from my face, I squint to make out the legendary castle and the little white lighthouse beyond it that signals the opening of the harbor, but all's still a blur.

Jamesy mutters, half-question, half-declaration, "So ye don't have oilskins then." A first cautious welcome. We're drenched and shivering in our thin city raincoats by the time the boat nears the castle. The tide is out, and the quay is tidal, so we must moor far out in the harbor and transfer our bags and ourselves into a small punt. Then Jamesy, huge-armed and silent, rhythmically rows us up the long harbor of this island we've come to live on.

The shock of its beauty stuns me. It's unlike anything I've known, and unlike what the mainland's starkness prepared me to expect: mountains, pastureland, bogs, sheer cliffs, sheltered turquoise bays, gardens, and glittering white sand beaches all share a single square mile, though like the mainland it's treeless. The land doesn't hold to any one hue for longer than a glance, the bleakest rock bordered with deep green grass, cliffs and boulders softened with moss, a tiny paradise plunked down in the midst of the sea like a gift. Greens and greys and boggy black-browns predominate, with the red of fuchsia and yellow of gorse—here called furze—competing for attention. How grateful the islanders must be for those perennial blooms. "When the furze isn't bloomin' the girls isn't kissin'," a local proverb notes. For blues, pinks, and purples, one must turn to the constantly streaming sky, or to the mainland where the range of mountains we traveled through now have no weight or color of their own, but are, rather, objects for the light to work on. They tower over sea level, bluing in and out of focus, permanent but shamelessly chameleon. Beyond them is the rest of Ireland. "Welcome to Ireland," the mainland locals sneer when the island boat ties up in Clochan. But the islanders care so little for the mainland they don't say they're going "in" to it; they go briefly, and rarely, "out."

Over there, across seven miles of unpredictable water: a country with a government, policies, police. Here: nothing but the island itself, largely left alone. We are free—freedom's the first thrilling sensation. We've journeyed over a divide to another realm. Even the birds are less afraid than on the mainland, allowing us to come close and stare. We've come to a world of heady, leisurely beauty where there are no laws, only courtesies and conventions. We are beyond the pale, beyond the clutches of the world, on the western edge, the Celtic fringe, for so many centuries the presumed end of the earth. The sense of isolation is marvelously acute, the deep silence unnatural to my ear, the rest of the world suddenly something to contemplate from a distance, or ignore. I am drunk on it, a natural for islomania.

It's drizzling at dusk as Harold takes us to meet our landlady. Harold is a painter and an old friend of

Owen's. Until today he was the only nonnative resident on the island, a pioneer. He arranged a house for us—a traditional island cottage with no electricity or running water—in a series of contradictory letters. He first reported that our rent would be four pounds a week and would include free milk and eggs. When we asked if a year-round agreement might bring down the price, Harold wrote back that the lady in question had agreed to 150 pounds for the year including milk, vegetables, and turf (dried peat from the bog, the only feasible way to heat). Harold advised he'd bargain further. His last letter, received the day before we left the States, announced a final offer of 100 pounds for the year—about 250 dollars—payable in two halves, with free milk, vegetables, and eggs. Harold said not to worry about the turf, although earlier he'd insisted it was an essential stipulation. These negotiated items are often in short supply.

All the houses look alike—grey rectangles of stacked local stone with painted shutters and lace half-curtains, smoke drifting somnolently from their chimneys now that the gale has passed. We're alone on the road. Harold's expansive with the pleasure of his task as guide, a stranger to the island himself a year ago, now expert and welcomer. He tells us the tale of how the island got its name: Two fishermen carrying a basket of hot coals (for cooking the fish they'd planned to catch) came to an impenetrable wall of mist. Investigating, they saw beyond it a beautiful young woman and a white cow. The cow's tail was swinging in and out of the mist, so one of the men grabbed hold of it and was swung inside. At that moment, a tongue of flame spilled out of his basket of coals and hit the ground. Fire being hostile to all things supernatural, the tail in his hand immediately turned to seaweed and the beautiful young woman turned into a hag. She cackled spitefully and dove into a lake. The mist sizzled clean and the island as it's now known was revealed. But the woman and white cow are said to return every seven years, and local tragedy inevitably follows their visitations.

Harold's gotten chunkier in his year here, Owen says, and grown a rugged island skin. He wears tall, muddy wellingtons, an unraveling Aran pullover, and his baggy pants are food-stained. His eyes dart possessively over the landscape as he reels off facts about everything we pass. The ruined barracks, the harbor's mouth, High Island, Friar Island, and Crow Island, three uninhabited lumps on the southwest horizon, and the two-room schoolhouse built in 1886—it educates the island children through sixth grade; at age twelve, they must go to boarding school sixty miles in on the mainland. There are only twenty-three children of grammar-school age at the moment, the smallest number ever, Harold says; the education's a joke, he adds.

We pick our way west on the high road—a road hazardous with holes, rocks, and manure—and the West Village, where Harold lives, comes into focus, a scatter of houses huddled between two hills beyond which the island ends.

I ask Harold if there will be any trouble about Owen and I not being married. Too raw in my memory is our experience last night on the mainland in a small town where we stopped for Bed and Breakfast. The matron blocked the door with her torso and glared. "Are ye man and wife?" she demanded as I kept my ringless left hand in my pocket. I muttered yes, but Owen pretended great offense and said, "Of course, madam," and got us the room for the night. I was shaken; fresh from the shelter of a university town, I hadn't anticipated the awkwardness of our situation and Owen had never warned me to be discreet. I had no interest in marriage, really, though prodded by friends once I'd gone to the library to find a book about Ireland in order to check on its divorce laws. Divorce wasn't even in the Index. That's because divorce doesn't *exist* in Ireland, Owen coolly informed me. He said a foreign divorce might be possible, but was I going to let legalities stop me in any case? Of course not. As for the island, Harold says confidently, "Not to worry"—islands are a world apart from Ireland's smug conservatism.

Our landlady is an old woman who lives with an unmarried son and an unmarried daughter midway between the Middle and West villages in a long, low house with bright red shutters. Inside it is bare but bright, its few pieces of furniture painted in crayon shades of all three primary colors. Though our landlady's given name is Mary, she's known as Rosie because of her unusually cheerful outlook and disposition. She's well over eighty, hearth-bound by arthritis, yet irrepressible. She wears her white hair in two fat braids that bob as she talks. "Yur very welcome," she crows from her armchair, smiling widely. "I'd stand up if I could, but I can't, so ye's sit down."

"Don't dream of getting up," Owen's quick to interject in that genial solicitousness that's his ready tone since he set foot back in Ireland.

Half-rising from a chair in a dark corner away from the fire, the spinster daughter, Ann, nods at us and mutters, "Yur welcome." A haunted figure half-veiled in a large kerchief, she's restrained, suspicious. Her timidity and bitter inwardness are unlike her mother's joyful curiosity. But Ann's the one who controls this kitchen in which things don't often go awry. She holds us off with her hard, cracked face.

But then her brother Sean bursts in through the back door, Sean who would come to be so dear to us, Sean so boyish and lovely, this first time we see him: the clear oval of his face, slim and mobile, his riveting aquamarine eyes, long distinguished nose, and wide heart-shaped smile lit with a laugh that explodes from his guts. Lean, nimble, he bounds toward us, dragging chairs from the kitchen table toward the fire in welcome. I was immediately taken by him.

But at that moment Sean was still a stranger, and who knows what passed through his mind at the sight of us—a cocksure, flamboyant, middle-aged man and timid young woman, both of us hopeful, enamored. "Sit down ye's, sit down," he shouts, brimming over with excitement. "Yur welcome indeed." Outside, the mountains wheel again, changing color, shape.

We stand off from the chairs, Harold protesting, "We'll only be a minute."

But—"Ye'll sit," Rosie insists, and so we do. Rosie, the weathered matriarch, lovingly bossy and gritty, but with a girlish, self-conscious giggle. "Sit up to the fire, ye, sit in." She makes Owen, guest of honor, take the padded armchair closest to the hearth while Harold and I claim small blue wooden chairs and form a ragged circle. Sean jauntily brings a chair over for himself, heady with eventfulness.

"Put on the tea, Ann," he glances at his sister in reprimand. She reluctantly starts to rise, but Harold and Owen both cut in, "No, we won't be stopping long," "Don't be troubling yourself," and she gladly resettles herself, studying us, invulnerable. I, for one, could use a cup of tea to warm up and am disappointed that one refusal, contrary to Irish tradition, was enough to squelch the offer.

Owen turns hopefully to our official landlady. "Well, that's a fine-looking house you have above." Harold had already taken us to peer through the windows of our future home.

" 'Tis a fine house, it is so, though a bit of work wouldn't do it any harm . . ." she trails off, not to confuse the rhetorical with a concrete offer.

"It's fine as it is," Owen returns.

" 'Tis a fine ould house altogether," she trumpets back, and launches into a brief history: " 'Twas my uncle's house, my mother's youngest brother, Jimmy was his name, he died three years ago, God love 'im."

"The poor maneen," Ann mutters, stiffly uncrossing and recrossing her legs.

" 'Twas always a happy house," Rosie waxes, "ye know what I mean? There was always music in it, ye might say music was the furniture of that household, poor as they were, God love 'em, Jimmy himself he played the fiddle." She gets a hold on herself and regains her sense of the duty at hand: "I hope ye'll be very comfortable in it."

We assure her we will.

"And if ye want a bit of milk, though the Lord knows we don't have much of it, ye come here in the afternoon with a bottle after Sean's finished the milkin', and ye could help yurself to a few vegetables and eggs at the same time."

"That's very good of you, thanks very much." Owen can't help himself, charming her already, easing us into acceptance.

"Those hens didn't lay in weeks," Ann suddenly inserts sourly.

"What are ye sayin'?" Rosie demands, slightly hysterical.

Sean barks, "Shur there's nothin' wrong with those hens a little—"

"Not the *color* of an egg," Ann interrupts again. "God help 'em."

"Sure, never mind about the eggs," Owen the diplomat.

"There'll soon be plenty of eggs," Sean insists. "And yur welcome to 'em."

"You're very kind," Owen summing up.

"Ye'll have a cup of tea," Rosie reignites, reaching to put a hand affectionately on Owen's knee as we begin another obligatory chorus of "No thank you" and "We won't be staying long."

Then: "The boat's goin' out again," Ann proclaims, affronted, addressing herself to the harbor-view window. "Now what in God's name for on a dirty night like this? There must be visitors in Clochan, shur. It's not for any one of us he'd go out again." She turns back vehemently and warns, "That boat'll be the death of ye's." Harold shifts in his chair and stares into his lap.

"That's the way," Owen mumbles philosophically, breaking the dark hiatus.

Rosie pokes her cane at my bell-bottom jeans and asks, "What kind of trousers are those a'tall?" and Sean laughs, half-embarrassed for her, half-delighted at the opportunity to joke, "Didn't ye never see a sailor, Mammy?"

"Well, I never saw a girleen that was a sailor, mind ye, but ye learn something new every day, thanks be to God. Yur very welcome"—me and my bell-bottoms.

At a glance from Harold, Owen, with traces of trepidation, stands and shakes Sean's hand, expresses gratitude, then crosses the bare room to shake Ann's, and I follow suit. Nonchalantly, he puts an envelope with the fifty pounds in it for the first six months' rent on the yellow oilcloth-covered table. No one acknowledges it, but Rosie smiles as she lifts the big key off a hook on the mantel and slips it into my hand, patting it shut. "I'm very glad to have met ye's. The best of luck to ye's now."

"Good luck, good luck," Sean and Ann call after us, extra loud for the benefit of a neighbor passing. We've passed inspection.

"And if there's anything ye need," Sean quietly

adds as we reach the door, "don't be wantin' it. Ye know where to ask." He winks.

On the way out, I notice that the vegetable garden's in a shambles and that the hens are mangy and starved-looking. Across the road, though, in Sean's territory, the barn and larger fields are in good order. "The two faces of Ireland," Owen instructs: Sean, waving once more from the doorway, Ann's back fading into the unlit corner of the emptied kitchen.

There are 230 people left on this Island of the White Cow, down from 1,500 at the turn of the century, and several thousand before the famine. When I meet them on the road, they cock their heads briskly to the right and say, "Great day," or, "Desperate day," however the day may seem at that moment. No matter how morose-looking, they are invariably friendly. The men all wear anonymously similar threadbare dark suit jackets and peaked caps whether fishing, farming, drinking, or doing nothing at all. They have hands made huge by work, rough and brown with blackened nails. Their faces are dry and contracted, work-stunned and weather-stunned, but their eyes glisten and their smiles are childlike. Their lives have for the most part been bitterly poor and monotonous, but they're still willing to be surprised.

The women are part-shrouded in large kerchiefs tied tight around their chins. The older of them wear long, printed cotton dresses, the younger, polyester slacks, permanent press, from town. They hold their arms stiffly at their sides or fold them protectively over their stomachs, and cross themselves ostentatiously whenever they pass the church. Their mouths have hardened into fearful smiles, their hands are scarred from battling back weather from the insides of their houses. They can't meet the gaze of outsiders head-on.

Children are dressed in baggy hand-me-downs, knees and faces smudged with dirt. Not dressed warmly enough. They avert their faces and rush shyly by.

The island has two teachers, one priest, one nurse, one guest house, two pubs, and three villages—East, Middle, and West. There's a high road and a low road and three crossroads, none paved. Grass grows down the middle of them all and they're slippery with cattle droppings. Every household has a few cows and a little land to cultivate. The holdings are tiny, but this island's one of the most fertile in Ireland—no miraculous land-making out of sand and seaweed here (as is the case in the Aran Islands where the fields are paved with slabs of limestone and soil is laboriously handmade). Large tracts of the less useful land here is commonage, where anyone may graze his herds, while the good fields are fought over. When a man dies without blood relations to leave his land to, the family that cared for him through his final illness receives his land. Apparently certain families make an occupation of such caretaking in order to enlarge their share of good land, and let their poorer land go fallow with each new acquisition. But in the more industrious past, every inch of the land was used. On steep, rock-strewn hillsides, the scars of former cultivation are still visible—long welts beneath the grass that were once gravity-defying potato drills. There was little choice—a population more than ten times its current number somehow managed to live on and feed itself off this hemmed-in bit of land. Though of course they always depended on fish. Some households still have boats and do a bit of fishing for food, but as far as income goes, lack of incentive keeps most ashore. The lobsters have been largely fished out after years of grabbing, and there's not much money to be made on anything else. The fishing life was never easy. "This is a crag in the midst of the great sea," says Tomás O'Crohan of the Great Blasket Island, an island much like this one,

> and again and again the blown surf drives right over it before the violence of the wind, so that you daren't put your head out any more than a rabbit that crouches in his burrow in Inishvickillaun when the rain and the salt spume are flying. Often would we put to sea at the dawn of day when the weather was decent enough, and by the day's end our people on land would be keening us, so much had the weather changed for the worse. It was our business to be out in the night, and the misery of that sort of fishing is beyond telling. I count it the worst of all trades. Often and again the sea would drive over us so that we could see the land no more—a long, long night of cold like this, struggling against the sea, with often little to get. . . .

For years the Galway train daily shuttled fish from Connemara to town. But, Seán MacGiollarnáth notes in his history of Connemara, "the railway . . . ran alongside the Galway-Clifden road because, it was reasoned, the road engineer had found the most suitable levels. It avoided the populous districts, it brought no prosperity, no dividends, and it has disappeared." In 1873 there were fifty-two working boats on the island; today, less than a hundred years later, there are three.

The island is a poignant mixture of beauty and ruin. The air, unmarred by industry and washed by the sea, is thrillingly lucid, invigorating. Colors rise boldly or are muted with mist, and distances lose their measure as the light changes. As if a wand were waved, the realm remakes itself hourly. We float, free of definition. To be on an island is to know oneself as mere shape drifting in and out of view, to know one's slippery place in the world.

But in bleaker light, the land itself is undisciplined rock thrusting every which way. The fences that divide it veer contrarily over passionately disputed borders, snaking up and down the stony hills like a ragged Great Wall of China. The fences are makeshift—rickety, mortarless stone half-walls along the top of which are embedded chunks of rotting planks to hold up rusty barbed wire, tufts of sheep's wool snagged and quivering in it, blue sailing rope or plain white kitchen string tying up loose ends that have been pushed through hundreds of times despite the best intentions. The old inner springs of a mattress or an iron headboard here and there serve as ineffectual gate.

The island is littered with crumbling walls and ruined houses—the numerous sad remnants of a vanished population. Anything useful's been stripped from the abandoned houses: the wood, metal hearth chains, roofs. So they stand as stone shells, open to all the world, nettles and docks thriving where floors were, the yards and gardens a waist-high tangle of weeds. Many of the ruined houses are attached to those still lived in; some are kept up as barns. Our village is the worst, decay just barely held back from the working doors.

In ditches I find the half-rotted hull of a boat, a single oar, a cracked plastic bucket, rusty tin cans, candy wrappers. For the islanders, obviously, this is no oasis to be protected from the modern affliction of trash.

Close around the quay, a dozen boats, upturned on land, let rain through their keels and onto old lobster pots and nets beyond repair. Whoever owns these boats and their accoutrements is past the thought of fishing, or dead. But no one breaks the boats or pots up for wood scraps—they are, I suppose, sacrosanct relics of a busier time.

Given the enchantments of the landscape, it's easy to overlook the island's blights, including the dilapidated corners of the house we've rented. Like all the island houses, it's built of island stone, its walls about two feet thick. There are still houses with traditional thatched roofs, but most, including ours, now have slate roofs imported from the mainland, though many barns are thatched. There is little to praise in these houses, save the unobtrusive way they blend into the rocky landscape from which they've come. Inside, our house is cold, damp, severe, and draughty. It has four good-sized rooms and a "porch"—a kind of separate foyer that we'll turn into something approximating a bathroom. The traditional big kitchen/living room's in the middle, a huge soot-stained open hearth in it, high ceilings of bare wood, whitewashed walls gone greyish and peeling, and four windows on the southern side, just one on the north—this because the coldest weather comes from the north, and is guarded against by an unbroken wall; yet the prevailing and wickedest winds and rains are from the southern half of the compass, so the house is left susceptible to merciless beatings.

For furniture, there is a bed, a small painted cabinet for clothes, a handsome old-fashioned hutch (the "dresser") full of fine dishes (so I didn't need my poor broken heap after all), a kitchen table and chairs, two armchairs by the hearth, and a blackened gas stove. One room has a table which can be used as a desk. Owen has already claimed it and, with a steely discipline hardening his face, dubbed it his "cell." He's to build a desk for me to put in our bedroom. The fourth room, apparently unused for decades, drives us back with its damp.

The First Spring

The floors are bare cement with a few straw mats thrown around; on the walls, a half-dozen garish paintings bought in town—bleeding-heart Crucifixions, a Byzantine-like Virgin, the Pope, and a John F. Kennedy inauguration souvenir plate—all of which we take down at once (explanations to Rosie later); over the door hangs the traditional Saint Bridget's Cross, a spring celebrant fashioned from island straw, which we happily leave in place.

The house is on a steep hill in the very middle of the Middle Village above the harbor, surrounded by a hedge of large fuchsia bushes, their red bells glistening in the rain. "Tears of Mary" is what they're called in Irish, a row of full-time grievers. From our southern windows we can see the mainland, the sea between, and the harbor. From the single front window, the western expanse of the sea, and islands to the north like beasts asleep on the water. This island is in the middle of a group of three. The island to the south—its name in Irish meaning "Gentle One"—is uninhabited thanks to the government's judgment that its population had dwindled past the minimum to support a school. The remains of the population was resettled outside Clochan in sight of the "Gentle One." To the north is the Island of the Boar, a fitting name, we're told, for as gentle as the other is, that one is fierce, grueling to live on. Only eighty people do; they have no shop, no pub, no priest, doctor, or nurse—a degree of deprivation beyond even this island's.

Every man in the bar inspected us discreetly as we walked in with Harold, our sponsor. I was the only

woman in the room—a curiosity, but one they warmed
to in spite of the taboo against women in Irish pubs.
Even on the mainland, women are unwelcome in the
bar section of pubs, but may sit in the specially pretti-
fied "lounge," a system that my initial failure to grasp
caused awkward panic on several occasions in Dublin
bars.

Island women never come here to drink, but occasionally steal in to buy cigarettes or minerals (soda) in
as unassuming a way as they can muster, unseeing, un-
hearing, squirming up to the edge of the counter nearest
the door where the barman Richard's big red ear is suddenly, instinctively present and ready to receive their
whispered requests with conspiratorial tact; money is
handed over, the transaction completed but unacknowl-
edged. Little girls do pub business for their parents in
the same way, but with more uncontrollable excitement—stolen glances at the drinkers and excruciatingly
shy smiles if spoken to. Little boys who come to the pub
on errands are allowed to respond, be kidded, prepared
for a fuller life.

I am as much an oddity in the pub as the children, and the men treat me with the same assumption
of harmlessness—indulgently tender. I am no threat—
I belong to Owen, I'm not one of theirs. Their faces
circle me, ruddy and thick, in a haze of stinging tobacco
smoke, a dozen voices tossing off "Yur a Yank?" "Yur
very welcome," "Hope ye enjoy yur holidays now," "The
weather'll soon pick up, no bother to it." They smile,
shake hands, ask if I know their relations in Brooklyn,
in the Bronx. The island's public, communal face—
friendly, curious, helpful, proud. A cluster of men
hasten to make the facts of the island known. The harbor outside the door is the best on this coast, they
boast—three-quarters of a mile long, the water wide and
sheltering. And that's why so many have come—pirates,

painters, armies, saints, trawlers, poets, and now tourists. That's why, conversely, the neighboring island is a ghost island now—its treacherous harbor. They still come for the harbor—Norwegian fishermen fleeing storms for drink and dance, and French yachtsmen who trade bottles of wine for fresh milk.

Owen leans one arm on the bar, head tilted, relaxed, smiling, already at one with the island men, only his cap of white hair setting him off from the crowd of tweeds and dirty grey-browns. "Tell me this and tell me no more," he addresses the man beside him, and everyone in earshot laughs. "Yur askin' the wrong man if ye want a short answer," says one. "If he wants an answer a'tall," says another. "What is it yur wantin' to know?" the maligned man comes to life. "It's that castle out there," Owen twitches his head toward the harbor. Three twitches follow.

The first man says the castle is Spanish—and indeed it has a Spanish arch at its entry. The next says it's English, and the one after, a pirate's castle. They all say it's hard to get to, slightly separated from the arm of the harbor and cut off at high tide.

Harold watches as the island men absorb us, smiling when they repeat things he's already told us, and gratified by our quick surrender to the island's grip—a place original, unduplicated, with a touch of charmed unreality, a spot missed by the advance of Europe.

"Man oh man," Owen embraces Harold as we leave. "What a shot in the arm!"

Harold's proud. "One of the last places of its kind left," he boasts.

"I love it already," Owen shakes his head, moved.

Harold kisses me on the cheek and nods at Owen. "You've done the right thing."

As we shout good night to Harold and leave the bright, heady hub of the bar hand in hand, I'm overwhelmed by the moonless dark—a purity of darkness I've never known, undiluted by the light of cities. Only the lighthouse at the tip of the harbor past the castle shows with its wanly blinking electrically paced signal. A donkey inhales to bray and breaks the night like a sheet of glass. Hardly knowing where I am, I shiver with an uncannily powerful sense of place: here, the island; there, Ireland; beyond, an unknown continent.

"Watchman, what of the night?" What is this place when the last of the drinkers has gone to sleep, an island awash in weather and dark . . . *Qui vive?* A rustle in the hedge can be only one of several known things—wind, terrified sheep, benign cow, stray hen or cat, or at worst a rat, though they're said to inhabit only the tideline. No one comes or goes in the dark; dawn dependably reveals the island as it was.

Black-backed gulls patrol the harbor from low rocks. Today the water's glass-still, the day dull but dry. Not a breath of wind, silence encompassing miles. Even after nearly a week on the island, the landscape catches me unawares. It abruptly draws me out of myself; I empty and it replaces me with its unbridled passion of cloud and rock and water. It is wild but meditative, expanding but compact, always beckoning. I am repeatedly seduced. The island does something to me I can't explain yet. It overrides me. I feel the shift to new ground inside, a deep excitement, a silence waiting for voice, and a great peacefulness, even when the rain and wind abuse.

Today the weather is playing dead. I watch a few gulls take off toward the channel, noiselessly passing themselves over the mirror of water, one, two, three.

The First Spring

After they're gone and the water's face is empty again, I toss in a handful of pebbles because the poignant stillness is suddenly too much—it's making lines of poetry fly through my trance-cleared head, like Neruda's "I need the sea because it teaches me," and "Infinity was there to know." I have no words of my own yet for what the island will mean to me.

I'm loitering down here at the harbor waiting to gain admission to the closet-sized grocery next to the pub. This shop has no scheduled hours and is almost always closed. Getting into it depends on the mood of the man who owns both it and the pub, the man who tends bar day and night—Richard Walsh. He's the tallest man on the island, wears a baggy black suit shiny with use, and big polished shoes; he has thinning grey hair, a fist of a nose, and a wide, mottled face, beaten red. At times he's forbidding, at others impish. I have watched him raucously joking, goading full-timers at the bar, his whole body twisted with laughter. And I have seen him morose, trying to read a newspaper by the pub's dim window, sneering if someone comes in looking for a drink, or change, or admission to the shop.

There's not that much to buy in the shop anyway. It's so small that, as Sean says, "Ye couldn't swing a cat in it." And what's for sale is for the most part depressing. The islanders are devoted to convenience foods with a passion that only the long-deprived can muster. Canned foods are status. The shop is stocked with canned carrots though the fields are usually full of the real thing. Cans crowd the narrow, musty shelves: cans of peas, baked beans, peaches, pears, envelopes of instant mashed potatoes, and cans of corned beef, a form of meat closer in texture to Alpo than to the sandwiches of my youth.

Adapting to what's available in the shop is proving difficult. The only cheese is processed, orange-dyed stuff, sticky and flavorless. Fresh fruit is occasional and expensive. There are rashers and sausages for sale in the guest house, but we haven't tried them—they're way out of line with our budget. Having found no steady supply of vegetables and eggs, despite Sean's assurances, we are living mostly on potatoes, fish when we can get it, bread and butter, oatmeal, our quart of milk a day—rich, raw, thick with cream—and endless cups of tea.

For water, we go to a well at the bottom of the steep hill on which we live—a spring-fed well with beautiful, clear, cold water. When I remarked to a woman we met there how good I thought it was, she complained that it has too much iron in it and turns teeth yellow—I would see. (Pessimistic warnings daily alternate with encouragement.) We only draw water for drinking and cooking from this well—one two-gallon bucket a day. For washing water, there is a big rain-water tank at the back of the house. Inside, instead of plumbing, the house is decked with plastic, a colorful bevy of buckets and basins: a huge bucket-shaped container with a seat on it that's the chemical toilet; a big basin that's the sink; buckets for well water, wash water, and used water. Distinctions maintained by color coding and location.

Owen is in his element, boastful of his rightness in bringing us here. He has leapt into this life with such naturalness and joy that it's infectious and I take, with him, inordinate pleasure in every detail. He talks endlessly and with absorption about our new neighbors and the ways we'll organize our days here. Owen can talk as enthusiastically about the north bog dump's archaeology of island life as he can about Sean ("Your archetypal peasant-mystic—you can see it in his eyes") and strategies for lighting turf. We are like children dropped into a wonderland. Owen babbles, but I listen, stunned.

The enormity of the change I'm undergoing sometimes dizzies me. Two weeks out of college I find

myself thousands of miles from home in a foreign country, for the first time living out of a city or town, and for
the first time living with a man. Every hour is an adjustment—to Owen's shaping presence and constant guidance, to domestic responsibilities (I can hardly even
cook), to a population whose English I can barely understand, to a raw environment without even the buffer of
light switches or toilets, no friends, no familiars. All my
habits must be broken. Everything is strange and gets
filtered through Owen. No wonder I don't have much to
say yet. I wake up startled, not knowing where I am.

And I wake up so cold that I refuse to get out of
bed until Owen battles the damp turf with scraps of
paper and dead fuchsia branches. Even then, the thick
stone walls and floor hold the cold obstinately. Owen
teases me for my timidity ("Don't act like an old woman
of ninety"), but I remind him that I spent my life up to
now with central heating set in the "comfort zone" and
an electric blanket to boot—it's my body rebelling, I
counter, not my spirit flagging. I have no intention of
chickening out, but I can't transform myself in a week.
"The muse is a hard mistress," he intones virtuously.
He says the climate's good for me. He says I've never
looked more beautiful. Behind his proselytizing humor
he is nourishing, gentle, devoted. He means to help me
grow up, and he means for me to love the West of Ireland as much as he does.

For Owen, our way of life here feels normal. He
grew up not in the West, but in the even colder Mid-
lands, and though circumstances improved with the
years, he started out in a house much like this one. So
electricity, bathtubs, and thermostats will never seem
necessary or even desirable to him.

His coming here, I now understand, is a rebellion
with several targets: the urban, bourgeois, and familial
(the losses of which—his wife and children—he refuses to

speak or let me question, insisting that the price is his, not mine). His being here is also a deeply felt gesture as an Irish artist. In most cases, Ireland's artists and intellectuals, like Owen, have a "peasant" background and are first-generation city-dwellers; being educated and leading professional lives in Dublin, they fear to be seen as rejecting their rural pasts and fear being cut off from their vital creative sources. Many go back to live, at least for a time, in the countryside that nourished them, though not necessarily in their home counties. Their acceptance by the country people they go to dwell among is of the utmost importance to them—thus Owen's conscientious winning over of everyone we meet and his determination that we become assimilated here, made easy by the islanders' respect for the articulate. They are pushovers for his tales and pithy pronouncements, just as I am, and are delighted to compete with their own.

"Yur a great man altogether," Sean applauds Owen as they fish together for the first time and Owen tells the story of how once out in a boat off the Aran Islands he'd been trapped in fog and had given himself up for lost when suddenly, "I heard a voice. And the voice said to me: 'Owen, row west.' I heard it as clear as if you said it to me yourself and there wasn't a soul in sight. A clear, low, instructive voice, 'Row west.' Well, you may well ask how I knew which way was west by then, but I'd seen the current running from the north before, so I rowed west from it and didn't I land on a spit of rock at the far corner of the island just fifty yards short of where I'd have drifted into the open sea. I wouldn't have had a chance. Better men than I have been lost at sea in Aran." "Ah, shur, there's no man better than yurself for the talk!" Sean says. "It's a saint they should be callin' ye after hearin' the voice with your name on it."

The First Spring

Despite the difficulties of adjustment, my enchantment with Owen has grown to include this far edge of the world he's brought me to. Its sounds and smells and colors enthrall me. Its pace lulls me. I love its deep natural silences along with its human clamor, its solitariness along with its vivid community. Owen was right—this is the kind of experience I was secretly hungering for. The island offers itself in answer to all my vague, frustrated longings.

Sunday morning. The first bell tolls at 8:30. The bell is on a slight rise behind the church, big and rusty. One of the choirboys, scrubbed and dressed in his white soutane, pulls the rope. After, there immediately begins the stampede of mass-goers—islanders in groups of three or four, all trudging in one direction. Traffic. Twitch-of-the-head hellos to one another on the corner.

Sunday best is something of an improvement on daily garb: pressed black suits, polished shoes, and thin shiny ties, only the stylistic anachronisms and frayed white shirt cuffs pointing to poverty. The women boast lacy cardigans and mud-speckled stockings; for many this is the week's sole outing. Mass. The one island-wide meeting. The watered-down ritual in the imposing cutstone church by the harbor. I see more people in half an hour than I've seen all week. Some, unable to control themselves, glance into our windows as they pass. Are we up? Are we going? The first Sunday test of us strangers.

Everyone on the island goes to one of the two Sunday masses, the holier to first mass because as soon as the second one's over at noon the pubs open for the two liveliest hours of drinking of the week. Two hours of holiday till Sunday dinner.

We are the only ones left in the village this noon. No prayers, Sunday dress, or celebration for us. We talked it out and decided to set things clear at once. Harold doesn't go to mass, though he attends the post-mass session in the pub in his usual, non-Sunday garb. But, good puritan, I said I wouldn't feel right in partaking of the fest not having served time in church, and Owen agreed. The whole Sunday rite seems to be the line we should not cross. That far into the heart of island life it won't be possible to tread without compromising ourselves. We'll stake our separateness, Owen insists, and hope for the best.

Our absence will undoubtedly be noticed and criticized. The unconventional are not suffered gladly in Ireland. But Owen says the Irish always make exceptions for writers. Writers are the weird but wonderful ones they should condemn but whom they can't help but love. They seem to have accepted our not being married without much fuss. Islanders, unlike mainlanders, confined for life with those who don't conform, must be flexible in order to survive. Or so it seems to us as we tentatively take our place in a community with whose values we're largely at odds, but in which we nevertheless feel exhilaratingly free and welcome.

An important discovery: plump, white-curled Bridget runs a well-stocked grocery in the East Village. It is always open, being an adjunct of her house, and she likes nothing better than to stand and chat behind her makeshift counter. Her house is part of the horseshoe row of pastel dwellings arrayed around the white sand beach and clear turquoise water of the East Bay. The whole line of mainland mountains curves maternally beyond, fading from blue to mauve to lavender.

Sudden civilization, this village, compared to our battered, half-rotted one. The shutters are freshly painted and the windowsills graced with red and pink geraniums. Cheerful, thriving—or so it would have us believe. But true enough, its residents are the friendliest and most open-minded of the islanders. Higher up, farther west, the population huddles inside, continually struck at, with only the unrelenting reality of wind and water to shape them. But the East Village is the island's sheltered jewel. Here live the nimble of spirit and quietly wise, those formed by the mutability of the Connemara horizon: they like surprises.

Bridget is the village's leading citizen. She welcomes us with a firm handshake—she knows who we are—and proudly tells me at once that she's been to America and thinks it "a great country." Two of her daughters are married to Americans and living on Long Island. "They have beautiful homes there. I'd go in a minute if I could." Official policy statement. Then, sweeping her left hand around the lovely village, "Ye can have the lot!" A touch of bitterness tempered by her red-cheeked wholesomeness. Bridget's not had an easy life—her husband's been bedridden for most of the last twenty-five years; she raised six children single-handedly, in poverty, doing farm work as well as housework. "That man'll never die," she whispers half-joking, whole in earnest. "He's had the last rites three times already and he wouldn't go. I suppose he intends to live forever just to have me waitin' on him. But for him," she confides, "I'd be in America with my daughters this minute!"

Despite her domestic martyrdom, Bridget's shop is lively, clean, and bountiful. Village children dawdle

selecting three-penny candies. If they can't pay, she jots
the price down in a little red notebook, maybe to be
totaled and billed later, maybe not. For us, the shop is
full of delicacies—tubes of Italian tomato paste, fresh
oranges, whole-wheat flour, honey, batteries for the
radio, commercial "fire lighters" (the trick for igniting
that recalcitrant turf), candles, and Brillo pads. Civilization! Enthralled to have us as an audience, Bridget
chatters away about American products and conveniences—"Well, the grocery stores—I never . . . the
choices of things! And the machines they've got over
there! When my children was young I hardly slept a
night, I was all the time up bakin' and washin' clothes.
My daughters didn't bake a thing since they got to
America. They can buy anything!"

Bridget waits for me to join in her enthusiasm,
but I only offer wan nods and acknowledging "uh-huh"s.
What she reasonably longs for is everything I've just
escaped. I'm embarrassed, a little confused. The ferocity
of her disdain and hunger surprises me, an angry zeal
riffling her soft pink face. Despite misgivings, I buy a
comforting pile of items from her shop, profoundly
grateful, for the moment at least, for her passionate com-
mitment to consumer goods. Two weeks of bland food
and struggle have been chastening. She hugs me good-bye
and declares me "a grand girl, a grand Yank," winking
at Owen as if approving his prize. I'm touched by
Bridget's affection, but already wish I could shed my
American identity tag, provoking, as it often does, these
anthems to the "American way" just as I am enthusiastically trying to embrace an un-American way. The
longings of Bridget force me to come up with a good
argument against things like washing machines, which I
can't honestly do.

Halfway back to the Middle Village from Brid-
get's, where the steep road dips into a sheltered valley, we

visit the island's cemetery. In a natural sun trap, hugged by hills and freckled with wild flowers, it's the most serene spot on the island. Amongst its hodgepodge of modern graves and crumbled Celtic crosses is the ruin of the island's early monastery, Saint Colman's (founded in 667 A.D.), just the stone walls of the abbey still standing in a litter of rocks and fragmented relics. The islanders blame its defacement on the Commonwealth soldiers who occupied the island beginning in 1652. This is the island's oldest structure and one of its claims to fame. Though the islanders like to assume the ruin is the original abbey, it's most likely a reconstruction, the seventh-century wooden structure having inevitably vanished. It is certainly on the site of Saint Colman's original settlement, though.

Saint Colman, from his monastery in England at Lindisfarne, was the lead character in what's known as "The Irish Controversy," a feud centering on the proper date for the celebration of Easter. The English Church organization, backed by Rome, challenged Colman's unconventional practices. At the Synod of Whitby in 664, Colman was ruled incorrect, and immediately left Lindisfarne with his company of loyal monks, going to the island of Iona to set up a rival monastery.

But in 667, in further flight, Colman left Iona and came here to the Island of the White Heifer, as the Venerable Bede calls it, to continue his spiritual mission. Some think that he was born here, and was returning home. Another version has it that he brought his monks to the island in flight from pestilence, "so that there might be nine waves between them and the land, for pestilence does not pass beyond that. . . ." In any case, it was a good refuge, a "desert in the western ocean," as they say, backward and unbothered, far from rumors of innovation. Trouble developed, though, when the Irish monks of his company, delighted to be home, took to traveling around Ireland all summer to visit relations. The English monks were left to work the land, the Irish returning just in time to partake of the harvest. This understandably annoyed the English monks, and Colman finally felt compelled to move again. He took the Englishmen to Mayo and founded yet another monastery, leaving the island one to the carefree Irish. They govern the island spirit still.

There's no documentation of Colman's death or burial, but the islanders insist he was brought back and buried here. In any case, the monastery remained active for centuries; the Annals of Ulster records the deaths of its abbots through the fourteenth century. It's said that hundreds of students flocked to the island for tutelage during those years when all Ireland was known as the "Island of Saints and Scholars."

Old Mr. Joe Coyne of the East Village, unofficial island historian, tells this further story: When Colman's monks built the abbey, they quarried slates for the roof from the rockface above the site. Years later, when the abbey was abandoned, the slates were removed and taken to roof the castle. That roof, after sheltering pirates, soldiers, and imprisoned priests, was also abandoned, and in the nineteenth century the slates were brought back across the harbor to roof the Royal Irish Constabulary barracks that was built in the Middle Village. In the perennial flux of institutions, that edifice too eventually became obsolete, and in the twentieth century, a mainland man bought the site of the ruined barracks on which to build a house. But first he cleared the property and took the slates to his own home on the mainland. There he used them to pave his garden—"A desecration!" my informant cries. "Wouldn't ye wonder about all the things them stones have heard said?" he asks the sky.

I do wonder. I'm moved by the meager ruins of

this important abbey that sit unattended, unplaqued, half-hidden by nettles and double daisies. Such neglect is typical in Ireland, Owen says, given the abundance of ruins. And these two gables and low walls are not that impressive architecturally. But the abbey's arching door strategically and gracefully frames the undulating mainland mountains. Joe Coyne, inclined to share our obeisance, stays on, staring. "Shur, with a view like that, ye could live on one feed a day," he says. Standing in the remains of the monastery, groceries strapped to our backs, I imagine monks here 1,300 years ago, worshipful as we are before these same indomitable mountains. And I remember that starry-eyed description of Ireland Bede begins his history with and wonder what Colman and his English monks and I have all come expecting . . .

> Ireland, in breadth, and for wholesomeness and serenity of climate, far surpasses Britain; for the snow scarcely ever lies there above three days; no man makes hay in the summer for winter's provision, or builds stables for his beasts of burden. No reptiles are found there, and no snake can live there; for, though often carried thither out of Britain, as soon as the ship comes near the shore, and the scent of the air reaches them, they die. On the contrary, almost all things in the island are good against poison.

Sean, as expected, has quickly become ally and guide, replacing Harold as our chief assimilator. Harold's a little put out. Having arranged to bring us here, he expected, I suppose, to keep us under his wing. But I haven't warmed to him—he's domineering, opinionated, bullish—nor do I think he's warmed to me. Raised in England, Harold wears his Irishness with a surly pride. For Harold, even more than for Owen, the island is a symbol, a cause. But he takes less delight in it than we do, more concerned to explicate the symbolic value of he and Owen being here. Beyond his introductory advice and the fruits of his year's experience, Harold can't tell us much about the island itself. He's too self-preoccupied and alert to insults—he's already made enemies here. It's the heart of the island Owen and I hunger to know, and so we've naturally gravitated toward Sean.

Sean is both the jolliest and the saddest man I've ever met. His face is so expressive, so changeable, that he's almost unrecognizable when his mood turns. When he's happy, like the night we met him and many nights since in the pub, his smile is huge, his laugh contagious. Though cursed by unsatisfying toil and bitter women like his sister Ann, Sean looks for the humorous underside of island life. He leaps to storytelling, always has an anecdote or chapter of local history to pull out, contradicts, confirms, and embellishes to draw out the talk of others, makes an epic of an incident, a novella of half a remark.

Many of Sean's tales are at the expense of other islanders; affectionate enough, but behind the delight taken in others' minor misfortunes is a tinge of malevolence I've begun to recognize between islanders—an itchy jealousy and disparagement fed by convoluted family histories, old crimes and rivalries. In a land where poverty and the struggle to survive is a permanent fact of life, it's not surprising they should scheme and try to outwit their competitors. In the claustrophobia of island life, such human tendencies are intensified. Bitchiness is an art. "If blood wasn't spilled some time or other in a bit of a fight, sure people would hardly know whether they had any blood at all in their bodies, and they would never know that one man's blood isn't as good as another's," Pat Mullen has a character explain in his novel *Hero Breed,* about life in the Aran Islands.

" 'And isn't it?' asked Hugh.

" 'Indeed it isn't,' said Johnny, 'because some men's blood has a lot of water in it!' "

With Sean, the ridicule of fellow islanders is fairly mild and seems mostly for laughter's sake. Conversations veer playfully, illogically, questions get answered with another question, and the point is the medium, not the message. Last night Sean and the island's only capable carpenter, an East Villager nicknamed Michael Hammers, were talking about a young man missing from the pub:

Michael: "Isn't Brendan lookin' very grand these nights?"

Sean: "Shur, hasn't he put on a stone's weight since he quit the cigarettes? He could ate the head of a horse!"

Michael: "It's true *for* 'im. He's gettin' a very roundy face."

Sean: "Roundy? He has a face on 'im as round as the back of a loaf."

Michael: "Ah, shur, but the lad is wise."

Sean: "Well that's the God's honest truth. That fella's so wise that if ye burned him to ashes ye'd have wise ashes."

Michael: "And he's a dacent lad, a great worker altogether."

Sean: "Powerful! Brendan the Bullock they do be callin' 'im, and it do *rage* 'im to be called it!"

Michael: "I do love to see 'im raged."

Sean: "He's beyond in Connemara yet. He went

out to buy a donkey, a ram, and a bantam hen, he told me so himself. Can ye credit it? Brendan the Bullock/ Went out to buy/A donkey, a ram/And a bantam hen . . ." His voice collapses in laughter. "Have another pint, Michael, ye too, Owen, put your glass up there, what are ye drinkin'?" Though hard to spot on such nights, there is also a deep sadness and loneliness in Sean's life that he turns upside down with banter. Like a child or puppy, he continually searches out what will keep him delighted. But sometimes it doesn't work. The weariness of unvarying labor and minimal food and heat stiffens him. When he's sad, he won't open his mouth at all, sits motionless and stares at the floor or tranced into the fire.

We never know if we'll find him like that or at his gayest. But no one's been as helpful or generous as Sean in acclimating us to island life. He often takes Owen fishing in his boat, and gives him a share equal to what he takes home himself. Owen's also helping him cut turf so we'll have a supply of our own come autumn— Sean's short at the moment so we're having to scrape by. When we're out together walking, Sean gleefully acquaints us with the names and checkered histories of our neighbors, and the name and history of every rock and hill we pass. Just outside our house: "The Rock of Guarim" where a foolish man quarreled with Colman's monks and put six of them to death; their blood is said to rise from the rock on every anniversary of the deed.

When sudden capricious showers douse us, as is their wont in Ireland, we stop and line up our backs against a sheltering stone wall or in the lee of a barn and talk until the shower's passed and sunshine and rainbows follow. Even without a shower as incentive, the population constantly pauses to talk. We've learned volumes worth of information by joining these slow, ru-

minative conversations at the edge of the road. During
one such session, Sean told us the island's most heart-
breaking story, "The Disaster."

" 'Twas a calm night altogether, and the men
had gone out fishin' as they did every night those times,
five boats from the East Village and three from the
Middle, and they hit a good shoal of mackerel in no
time. So they was soon haulin' in the trammels loaded
with fish—those times there was no shortage of fish, not
a bit of 'em. Anyways they were haulin' in the trammels
when out of nowhere, faster than a shark can flick his
tail at ye, the wind whips up and they was in a hurricane, honest to God they were. Well, there was never a
thing like it seen here before or since, the boats was
kindlin' wood in minutes and all the people in the
East Village could see it happenin' from the shore,
standin' there watchin', not a thing in the wide world
they could do, God bless the poor divils. Twenty-five
men from these waters was drowned that night. There
was only one man saved his boat and crew, the greatest
seaman there ever was on this island, and his name is
Stephen Mannion—he's alive yet, ye'll meet him some
night now in the pub when the weather improves, he's
too old to be wanderin' about in these showers.

"Mine own uncle was in the boat that Stephen
Mannion saved—Sean's his name, 'twas for him I was
named, Sean Ginger we do call him on account of his
red hair. Well anyways, what Stephen did was to keep
his nets full of fish. All the others cut away their nets,
ye see, tryin' to save themselves, but Stephen knew the
weight of the fish was what would save his boat, and
more power to 'im, 'twas the God's honest truth too.
They worked the oars against the wind for seven hours,
Stephen and Sean did, while a ladeen they had with 'em

held the nets, and ye can be shur that was the hard work. After seven hours at it, there was a break in the wind and they rowed flat out and came into that little strand I was tellin' ye's about where there's cockles to be had, and they were sound then, right enough. Well, now, thems in the village thought that none of the boats had a chance and they'd keened the whole fleet and all the men in it and they were in a terrible state altogether. My father was standin' by our front door cryin' over his brother when doesn't he see Sean himself, Stephen, and the ladeen (he's dead since in England, that one), doesn't he see the three of 'em walkin' down the road toward the village, and he cries out to them, 'Stay back,' because ye see 'twas ghosts he thought they were. He ran inside straight away and bolted the door against 'em, the poor divils. Well, Sean Ginger comes knockin' at the door because he was stayin' with us that time in the back bedroom, and my father says, 'Go away,' and Sean Ginger says, 'What are ye sayin'? 'Tis alive I am.' ' 'Tis dead ye'-are, 'tis only a ghost ye'are,' my father shouts, and Sean shouts back, 'I am not, 'tis alive I am, I'm tellin' ye,' and my father was shakin' like a leaf in a gale by now, I can remember it clear as yesterday. He shouts again, ' 'Tis a ghost ye'are, go away with ye now and that's the end of it.' So anyways, Sean gives up knockin' at the heel of the hunt and sleeps in the barn that night with the cows and horses. Could ye credit it? After all the poor man went through and 'im spendin' the night in the barn? 'Twas a great tale often told afterwards, that, Sean sleepin' in the barn after survivin' The Disaster. But shur, 'twas only the three of 'em in it that was saved from the whole fleet, twenty-five men dead and gone, God rest their souls."

The shower stopped, but Sean still stood and stared at the sea somberly.

The First Spring

I waited for his grief to ease. "When did The Disaster happen?" I asked him quietly.

"Nineteen twenty-six," he said.

He'd told the story with such fresh pain in his voice that I was shocked. How many dozens of times had he told it before? He could only have been a child when it happened.

All such stories remain contemporary in the island imagination. Past lives perpetually retold, in pub talk, in talk for outsiders, become present lives that people the monotony of fish and hay and potatoes. Stories are told to document, with pride of hardship, or just for the love of stories, for there is nothing in the stories themselves to love. They are all disasters—wrecks, drownings, abuse at the hands of various governments. The islanders rise to disaster like moths to a flame, often burned, but unable to resist its vivid attraction.

I asked Sean do people still believe in ghosts as his father did. "Ah, shur, they do and they don't. The priests don't have no truck with 'em." And what about the fairies? "That's a trap of nonsense altogether." But I'd heard him once explain the loss of the wheel of a cart to the meddling of the Little People. "Well, Deba" (what my name has turned into here), "I'll tell ye this. I'd say there are some things ye couldn't explain if it wasn't for the fairies to blame 'em on. But shur, the priests have the upper hand of 'em now. I didn't see no fairies round here in a long while."

As day to day we walk, take shelter, and listen, the island tells us its history, tales, and superstitions. I've grown to admire the islanders' characters tremendously— their hardness and skill coupled with a natural openness and playfulness. They are shaped by the duality of the landscape they live in: the immediate harshness of rock and damp which governs their lives, and the ethereal vista which feeds their spirits. The capricious sea, unremitting rock, and insubstantial bog constantly assert their authority and make them humble. "The tide waits for no one," Jack wisely salutes the sea as he rushes travelers on deck.

But safely on land, rules are to be challenged—the drama of dispute's what's relished, not the value of a common code. Depending on his mood, Sean will insult the Church in one conversation and praise it in the next, leaving himself indefinable. All one can be sure of is the pleasure he takes in talking. Even the children constantly display their parents' lively, anarchic doubt—I heard two sisters arguing over what time their favorite radio show came on: "Mammy said 'twas five." "She did not say five." "She did so." "She did not. And what's five anyways? Only a number."

Only the pronouncements of the Church hold sway, and tenuously enough in daily life. It's the prehistorical burial cairns atop mountains that catch their eye and talk in passing, not the artificial flowers ensconced in cross-shaped plastic boxes that adorn the recent graves. Native lawlessness is the mad spark in the islanders' eyes that I am drawn to, their readiness to pitch the rule book out the window and weave jokes about it for the rest of the night. It's the mad spark in Owen's eyes that I was drawn to, too, what makes him so much at home here. He and Sean are as untamable in their forties as my friends and I try to be in our twenties. They make it possible to believe in the ageless land of the fairies lying, by tradition, beneath the sea nearby.

Today Sean took us to the beach where thousands of cockles flourish under an inch of wet sand. Armed with rakes, we methodically worked a row each in the invisible boundaries delineated by Sean; an hour's work filled our bucket with dozens of fat cockles—a feast of free food—but you have to know the right spots. Sean's proud to have been the revealer for us, that's the kind of man he is.

While we enthusiastically raked, listening for the music of metal hitting shell, Sean told us that most of the islanders don't bother with cockles—raking threatens their prestige: they'd rather buy one of the frozen chickens that occasionally turn up for sale at the guest house just to prove they can afford them. Shellfish remind them of the famine, Sean said, as if they'd all personally lived through it. But maybe it's all more memorable than I suppose. Men point to a small graveyard just beyond the borders of the West Village where western famine victims were buried. Survivors were too weak to carry the dead a mile and a half east to the island's main cemetery. They call this burial plot "The Children's Graveyard."

A fisheries inspector's report of exactly one hundred years ago said of the islanders: "Many of the people . . . , very many of them, have nothing to put in the ground. . . . In one house I found them eating their dinner, which consisted of boiled seaweed, with limpets in it." Sean's father, in any case, always said that cockles were "a great feed," and that three cockles were "the equal to one egg." His father was from the mainland—a Connemara man—and so had an unjaundiced view of such matters.

Sean, like a disproportionate number of the male population here, is unmarried. Puritanism, economic obstacles, and cultural tradition conspire toward a straitjacket of asexuality. The waste is distressing—so many fine men wandering the roads alone, nothing to go home to. Of course the culture makes a joke of it—"It's better to spend yur life wantin' what ye don't have, then havin' what ye don't want." It's easy to see how hard it must be to create a life of one's own in this place. Building a house is not often possible in the circumstances, and a man must stay with his land. To bring a bride, successfully, into one's mother's home depends largely on the generosity and good will of the mother. And the Irish mother tends to reserve an exclusivity for herself—an end-of-life revenge for lifelong powerlessness, a final reign as widowed queen. Her sons honor her, all too often, by not bringing home rivals to her female authority. And so they wither, loveless. Rosie seems so affectionate and open, but who knows what darkness lurks behind that brightly painted kitchen which also produced an Ann.

It's an odd feeling that I've come to enlarge my life in a place where people can rarely escape the most curtailed and prescribed of existences. I've been rereading Patrick Kavanagh's "The Great Hunger," that epic poem about men like Sean.

> Maguire was faithful to death:
> He stayed with his mother till she died
> At the age of ninety-one
> She stayed too long.
>
> . . . .
>
> And he is not so sure now if his mother was
>   right
> When she praised the man who made a field his
>   bride.
>
> . . . .
>
> Lost in the passion that never needs a wife . . .
>
> . . . .
>
> Where eunuchs can be men
> And life is more lousy than savage.

Almost every family on the island is on welfare—"the dole." Without the dole, they could not live. But that's not quite true—they always lived without it before. Much more industriously, less comfortably. One generation back there were weavers and tailors; clothes were not imported, nor sails for the boats, not to speak of engines. Women carded, spun, and knit the island wool. They reaped their own grain; no hundredweight sacks of flour from the mainland. They cooked and heated by the open fire; no gas stoves, no portable oil heaters. The only money to make was by fishing. With money one could buy a watch or a radio in town. Life was harder, longer-houred, and even more limited and routine. But one can't help feeling, looking at the best that remains in these people, that it was pristine, that it carried the rhythm of countless generations with it, and had the weight and grace of necessity. As an old man in Maurice O'Sullivan's *Twenty Years A-Growing* comments:

> Upon my word, . . . it wasn't too bad for that time. There was no flour to be bought, no tea or sugar. We had our own food and our own clothes,—the pick of the strand, the hunt of the hill, the fish of the sea and the wool of the sheep. The devil a bit was there to buy, . . . save tobacco, and you could get a bandle of that for threepence. So where was the spending?

Of course, some went to England even then, those who wanted more. And news of their rewards filtered home.

Today's situation is a painful compromise, a straddling of the new and old worlds, both incomplete, the whole thing a tease and a trap. The dole doesn't provide enough to lead a modern life. Yet modern life bombards the island daily in radio advertisements and in the talk of visitors, and there is no room for more than two or three to make a decent income here. The industriousness of years past is now a symbol of poverty, humiliation. Polyester is a great convenience; there is

no weaver on the island anymore. When each head of
household lines up at the post office on Friday to cash
his government check, he buys a few sweets for the children and walks home with a pocketful of money he
hasn't earned but surely deserves, a pocketful of money
that goes nowhere toward meeting his aspirations.

Most single men drink the dole. Night after
bland night, Sean and his bleak counterparts sit in the
pub as the only relief from field work, cows, and an
often empty house. Some have gape-mouthed looks of
stupidity, their faces lost somewhere, irretrievable;
others, like Sean, are afire with untapped intelligence.
They are all, though, the ones who stayed, the ones, perhaps, less driven to achieve, the ones more loyal to family,
the more passive ones waiting for opportunity to land in
their laps, or those, simply, more attached to home.
They've watched comings and goings and have stayed on;
they know much doesn't change, no matter how much
seems to change. Knock-kneed and bent, they've been
kicked back a thousand times.

Most of the women have left. The women who
couldn't marry at home have married in London, or a
lucky few in America. They write home enviable letters.
They have baby-sitters and dishwashers. The women
who stayed without marrying did so to care for parents
and are useless and bitter when the parents die.

The men drink away the day's wages of poverty
nightly. What do they need money for anyway? The dole
is a good deed then, a kind of anesthesia. Or the dole is
the curse that's broken the spiritual back of the place,
more deadening than centuries of colonialism. The dole
is humiliation. The dole is not enough. The dole is the
least the government can do.

There is a woman in our village who stays up
until three or four in the morning most nights washing

47

clothes for her nine children. I wake up and see row on row of small clothes flagging the morning sun, whether in victory or defeat, I cannot say.

All the island children have badly decayed teeth. Their diets are inadequate and too often cookies or candy are bought instead of meat or eggs. A dentist comes in once a year to pull the teeth that are rotting. Most adults wear false teeth.

When Sean stares at the floor and will not tell a story or laugh, I think what a loving father he could have been, how warm he is, given an outlet. He is nearly fifty.

One can look at island life as cruel and ugly. But that's not my inclination. What is beautiful in this island's life is the spirit it has held on to in spite of centuries of adversity, the joy a good story is told with, the pleasure taken when the potato flowers bloom, when a storm clears and the sea goes table-still, when the children put on their Easter show and sing and dance as all children do.

When Saint Patrick viewed this region from the peak of the pyramidic mountain to the east that's named for him, he blessed it and promised it riches. "Where are the riches?" the doubtful may well ask. "In the people," is what the Connemara storyteller replies.

Our daily routine has become strict and fine-tuned. So many essential tasks must be done each day that there's little allowance for bad moods or procrastination; fortunately we both thrive on such demands, and that rhythm helps give our days purpose. There's well water to be fetched each morning, the hearth to be swept clear of ashes, the fire started and tended to, the slop bucket and toilet to empty, wash water to replenish, water to keep hot on the fire, oil lamps to be filled, the milk to be collected, bread to be baked, the trash to be carted, kindling to be gathered, shopping expeditions to the East Village, and loiterings on the quay to get spare fish when the boats come in. We've forged habits and established an easy routine of early-morning chores and breakfast, then five or six hours when we each write, then late-afternoon chores and dinner-making. At night we either read by the fire or go out to the pub. The balance is perfect: uninterrupted, silent solitude for work, a quiet I can dredge my truest self from, and the good busyness of necessary chores, active, physical, satisfying.

Curiously, the islanders keep altogether different hours than we do. They stay up well past midnight and sleep till eleven often. The cows don't get milked till noon, then not again till nine or ten at night. Even schoolchildren stay up till midnight and don't have to be at school until half-past ten or so. We are usually the first up in the village, terrifying sheep as we go down the hill to the well, scattering birds fitfully—the first disturbance, the start of day. Only one old man at the hill's bottom is also sometimes up—the man known respectfully from his seafaring days as "The Captain"—just lighting his fire, the smell of his turf smoke startlingly pungent on the unspoiled morning air. The rest of the islanders we don't see evidence of till afternoon.

For all the apparent isolation one can make for oneself, village life is still fairly public and there are certain assumptions about what people will be doing at certain times of the day that we don't observe. We don't have our dinner at one in the afternoon, for instance. And we've happened, on occasion, to make love in the middle of the afternoon, a risqué and risky act. We were, in fact, discovered at it one afternoon by Sean who, as is the custom, walked in without knocking and was struck mute with embarrassment. All aspects of island behavior are governed by customary patterns that we don't for the most part fit. Inside the house I forget those strictures, but outside I find myself conforming, already, to certain codes in order to spare others discomfort, particularly in relation to Owen—it's best to pretend we're not much interested in one another. Men and women move in separate circles here, never as couples. Sex is dark and private.

The island's weekly schedule is as rigid as the daily. Saturday is bath day, hair to toenails, for the sabbath. Late Saturday nights behind drawn drapes, water is boiled, basins dragged out, and children forced to stand in them, shivering. Bathing has been our most difficult adjustment. I couldn't bear to wash in the cold privacy of our so-called bathroom as I suppose most adults do. It's the kitchen fire for me—I park a basin right before it and pour in two boiling kettles' worth of water and carefully add the cold. Then I move fast, shrieking when the cold air smacks me, and leap around in mock agony while I dry myself off. Luckily we don't have to bathe or wash clothes as often as I'm used to; the air is so clean we simply don't get dirty. Luckily, because laundry in particular is a major production of water hauling, boiling, and dumping that takes a full morning's work.

The other adjustment I've found difficult is lack of news, our only, limited source being the radio—or the "wireless" as they call it here, still marveling at its mysterious abilities. The single radio station—Irish national broadcasting, run by the government—is a potpourri of talk, pop music, traditional Irish music, weather reports for landlubbers and weather reports for fishermen, weather reports and programs in Irish for no other reason than the fulfillment of a quota set in hope of saving the rapidly dying language, an occasional classical concert, a weekly theatrical hour, a daily soap opera religiously followed by thousands, a nightly cattle report (a bovine-voiced recitation of the price per pound of Herefords and Charollais at village fairs around the country), a nightly report of traffic conditions in Dublin, and a nightly recipe, chosen from listeners' contributions, for "tea"—the traditional light evening meal—all of which rely on rashers, potatoes, and finely chopped onion sautéed until translucent. Not much time for world news.

The paucity of contact with the outer world takes a calm resolve to yield to. The mail only comes four times a week, three in winter—though that's something of a joke, Harold admits, because in the winter we'll be lucky to get it once a week. He didn't tell us, slyly, before we decided to come, how bad the gales get, how the boat is often laid idle a week or two at a time during the winter. But winter's a long way off . . .

Jack and Jamesy bring the mail bag in on the boat and haul it up to the post office where the postmistress and postman, another Sean, nicknamed, not surprisingly, Sean the Post, sort it. Sean the Post is a lean dark man of fifty. He makes the round of deliveries on his bicycle, snaking miles around the island, out peninsulas to houses secluded on spits of rock, and back again, a five- or six-hour door-to-door task. Already we await the mail passionately, it being our only palpable connection to the rest of the world, and our only source of money. Once the boat arrives, we're on high alert, waiting for the sound of Sean's bike to fall against the gable, the creaking gate, his footsteps, the pungent smell of his damp leather mail bag.

I watch and listen for him from the northern window. On the uncannily clear days before rain, our neighboring islands are shoved up close beside us—the

Island of the Boar, seven miles north, a reach away, two houses plainly visible on its southern slope. Exact-edged and blue, Achill Island puckers the horizon beyond though it's dozens of miles to the north. Achill, famous for its cliffs and views, has paved roads and a bridge to the Mayo mainland—hardly a real island at all anymore, now that there's a route for quick influences. The thrill of islands is their separateness, the necessity of a special journey to reach them, and the special sense of isolation once there. "What pleasure," an old saying goes, "to be enclosed on an island." "What it comes down to eventually," writes Jerome Kiely of Clear Island, "is that Ireland and the island are two quite different places. It's like the relationship between the earth and the moon: one is a satellite of the other, but the atmosphere is quite different; it is much more rarefied on the moon." "The story of the Achill boy who wrote in his geography lesson that Ireland was a large island lying off the coast of Achill may be apocryphal," comments Gratten Freyer, "but it reflects a feeling one gets when one is there." It is even more the feeling here.

Our neighbor P.J. passes the northern window riding his donkey side saddle. He hits the dawdling animal's rump with a broken-off rod and growls, less in hope for speed than in ritual. Another neighbor, Jim-John, walks back and forth from his barn to his fields to his house, first east with an empty burlap sack hooked over his shoulder, then west with the sack full of hay or potatoes or God knows what, the load's weight or lack of it making not a jot of difference to his gait, bent and slow.

So many Jims on the island that this one is identified by his father's name as well, a spontaneous system of patronymics. He is a gentle and generous old man, this Jim-John—he sold us a big sack of potatoes shortly after we arrived, half a hundredweight or more, and all he'd take was ten shillings—fifty pence in the new money, which they deign adjustment to—about a dollar twenty-five. Since then he's been a warm acquaintance and has promised us carrots and turnips come summer.

From the northern window I also observe our nearest neighbor, a single woman, scurrying back and forth on the road. She walks twice as fast as I can, her whole body thrust forward, projecting herself into the next chore, the next hour. I can't imagine how she gets up the hill so fast with a bucket of well water in one hand and a grocery basket in the other, and how she doesn't need to rest after. She's over seventy. As thin as a girl, she's always wearing several layers of sweaters and a big black wool coat no matter what the temperature. Coattails fly after her like wings. She mutters to herself as she flies.

The couple of times I've almost met her, by collision, she's avoided my look and spurted away. I've deciphered only a word or two from her constant stream of mumbling—"Ooooohh . . . heavenly bless tonight . . . yes, yes, God love ye!" Then she's gone. All we'd learned about her until today is that she lives alone, across the road from us, and that she's named Theresa. Her drapes are always fully drawn.

This morning when we opened the door, a big bag of turf fell into the porch. I asked Rosie when I went for the milk if Sean had dropped it off, but she said no, and squinted conspiratorially, resolved to identify the donor. She said she'd make "inquiries."

Then on the way back, I found myself in Theresa's flight path as she rounded the village corner. "Well, heavenly bless tonight," she gasped at me. "Ye'll be wantin' a better fire these evenings. I don't see much smoke comin' out of that chimney of yurs. Isn't *she*—the syllable stretched malignantly—"givin' ye's any turf?" Before I could answer, Theresa was gone.

The First Spring

I was mightily impressed. Generosity banded to curiosity and condemnation of a fellow islander, an oblique attack coupled with charity. I thought to go and thank her outright and bring a reciprocal gift, but Owen said I was being too damn American, intolerably direct, and would embarrass her. Some subtle, appropriate acknowledgment would occur to us, he said, in due course.

Why, despite the number of difficult adjustments, do I already deeply love this at times unlovable place? Curiously, the islanders are much more determined to get an answer to that question than I am. "Why would ye be comin' to a place like this?" I've been asked a dozen times, not with any lack of welcome, but with genuine bafflement—if I'm crazy enough to want to stay, that's okay by them. The questioners are invariably friendly, but why, they hunger to know, give up white-tiled bathrooms, cars, central heating, and "fil-ums" (they are all mad for movies) for this? The first few times I was so questioned, unprepared and spellbound, I praised the island's unique beauty and simple, slow life which has so captured my affections. But in this they saw only fodder for self-deprecation. "Shur, there's nothin' suitable for a lady in these parts." Lady?

Only one of my responses has had any credence—my praise of the quiet. So this I have let suffice. Love of the quiet they understand from brief visits to towns and working stints in England. The noise and pace of city life is a thing beyond most of their adaptive powers. "I suppose a writer needs a quiet place to work, that's for shur."

A quiet place. There are no train whistles sounding in the night on the Island of the White Cow. Not even a foghorn or ship's whistle. No leaves to rustle. A moo in the dark startles. Footsteps on the road—I recognize the walk, the shape of the back: "Good night, Pat."

"Good night." The island's four cars and two tractors—we can hear them coming from a mile off and by now can identify them by the sound of the engine. Maura's Austin Minor heading back east from the bar at three in the morning, so loud it wakes me like an explosion.

In all those "why"s there was wariness too, at first, of us as writers—have we come to write a book about them? In those first days, the idea of ever writing about the island seemed far-fetched, the last thing we would want to do. Embracing their lives, how could we stand far enough back to describe them? We were in love with them, protective and respectful. Whether they intuitively knew that, trusted us, or couldn't resist in any case, they began without encouragement to tell us their stories and confide their secrets—all the wrongs that had been done to them by other islanders: land swindles, house swindles, bog swindles, public insults, innuendos, downright lies. In truth, they long for ears to pour their secret grievances into, even after having been burned by, of all people, a former priest who twenty years ago wrote a mercilessly gossipy book about his stint on the island—how no one had a kind thing to say behind anyone else's back, how they all detested Joe Coyne and his interminable stories, how bees had singled out and plagued the single island atheist, which of the women had been pregnant before they got married, and so on, an unloving catalogue of the island's worst features. It is still a source of rage.

Back in 1920, another priest wrote of them:

> They are a guileless, friendly, unsuspecting people—sometimes overmuch so, for there have not been wanting occasions, which they justly resent, when cynical and high-sniffing pundits have been received by the islanders with open-hearted, cordial kindness and wel-

come, and afterwards they were rewarded by publications which poked fun at their religious observances, traditions, customs and beliefs.

It didn't surprise me one night when a man in the pub, drunk and bubbling over with a malicious story about his neighbor, suddenly drew himself up and asked, "Yur not goin' writin' this down, are ye?" I reassured him. But there's such respect for writing, such desire, even at the cost of one's privacy, to have one's story told, that the stories pour forth anyway. As a recent anthologizer of stories about islands, Proinsias O'Conluain, says, "It's a very deprived Irish island indeed that hasn't had at least one book written about it." The men say, "This is a great place for the crack [talk]," and, "Ye've come to the right place for stories." That isn't why we've come, but clearly the longer we stay, the more hearts will be opened to us, the more stories we'll become the caretakers of. No one here, with their appetite for being jilted, really does believe we will stay, though.

We can only stay if we make things work economically. Of course there's no money to be made here. So Owen has arranged free-lance work in Dublin and has begun to get a first few assignments for me too. Book reviews, articles, radio scripts, all of which we can handle through the mail. Harold says once the rent is paid, we should be able to get by on five pounds a week, twelve dollars and fifty cents. But that means eating mostly what's here for free—fish, potatoes, vegetables in season— and living as stringently as Harold does. And it means ignoring threatening letters from bank managers and income tax men that have followed Owen from his marriage. He writes them loftily about the life of the artist and says, "I haven't the nails to scratch myself with, Sir." Given that we're barely scraping by, these old debts are, to me, a terrifying specter I can't imagine our banishing. As with all the specters of his past, if it bothers Owen, he doesn't let on.

We didn't save as much money in advance as we'd hoped. We arrived with seventy-two pounds, fifty of which went toward the first six months' rent. We've yet to receive any checks in the mail.

The West Village looks like a movie set for a marginal hamlet. Isolated, medievally stark, it is the most forlorn-looking spot on the island—set into the backsides of cliffs, its road a mess of loose stones, its houses too far from one another for neighborliness, sullen and ill-kempt. The village rises until its last house disappears behind the island's final outpost of green. Donkey-drawn carts come down with empty sacks or empty gas drums in them, heading toward the quay for filling. The men here are not used to strangers, or to having to speak—tourists don't usually come any further than the pub at the foot of the village. Life farther up is forbidding. The West Villagers are a completely different breed from the other islanders, self-contained, impenetrable, the most resistant to accepting outsiders. This is where Harold lives and it's taken him an entire year to penetrate their defenses. They, after all, are the ones in the teeth of the prevailing gales—they're hit first, they take the brunt, and are used to turning their backs. They've shunned improvements the other villages have been quick to take to—they have no grocery, their one phone is almost always out of order, and as a final indignity, they're at the end of the mail route. There are no children playing in the road as we walk through the village. A few washrags flap on a clothesline. It's startling how different this is from our own village—another tribe just over a mile away; two and a half miles away, the East Village is another universe.

Harold's assimilated himself into island life with the West as his model. He spends most of his days and nights here and has blended in well with its harshness and suspicious reticence. His house is depressing—dirty, with almost no furniture, and no decoration of any sort. It lacks all conveniences, any amelioration of hardship. He doesn't even use a chemical toilet, but a chamber pot and the barn instead. Harold endures the worst in things as a matter of honor, adheres to island deprivations with a religious fervor. He has weaned himself of all pleasures but drinking, which he does quite a bit of. Increasingly, he seems to vaguely disapprove of us. Hardship is a virtue in Harold's book, and he finds our small relieving luxuries (a wheel of decent cheddar cheese ordered by phone from Clifden, to be rationed out for a month) distasteful.

Because of this tension between us, we seldom join him here to drink. And anyway the pub in the West Village, like the village itself, is far less appealing than the one by the harbor. It only opened a couple of years ago, and to compete, it breaks the law—the law of the land (Ireland) being an 11:00 P.M. closing time for every bar in the nation. Richard, at the harbor pub, keeping to the spirit of the law of the land, closes his pub at midnight. Jim, in the West, keeps his open till two or three in the morning. Thus, at midnight begins a migration west of all hard-core drinkers and hangers-on.

The men stand or sit in an awed stupor, uniformly clad in dark caps and jackets, their faces flushed with drink or virginity, holding fat pints of stout in their left hands as lovingly as they might the hands of women. In their right hands, between thick calloused finger and thumb, they hold cigarettes, lit side to the palm. From time to time they flick ashes off onto the floor and twist their hands up to take deep draws. The cloying smell of strong tobacco muddies the air. Some men throw their heads back into it, talking loudly. Most stare at the floor and peer out occasionally sidelong. All offer cigarettes around whenever they take out their packs (the donor alternates, just as with rounds of drinks) so there's an ambience of generosity and communal spirit, but of course the tally is furiously kept in mind and carried over one night to the next, one year to the next. "Sit down, daughter." An old man stumbles up to offer me his seat and nearly falls over on me as he tries to move aside. I overhear: "Have ye anything left a'tall? . . . Ye couldn't buy a feckin' pint! Sorry missus," (to me) "I didn't see ye. Ye couldn't buy a pint!" A less polite pub than the harbor's.

Sean's brought us to hear a young man who plays the melodeon. Not very well, Sean admits, and he only knows a few tunes, but they're good ones. Well into the night at Jim's, when enough pints of stout have left creamy rings on the formica-topped tables and moustaches on the upper lips of voluble men, Will is begged, chided, commanded, cajoled into taking out the melodeon. "Naa, leave me be," he barks back, plastered. But in any case, protest is *de rigueur*. "Ah, give us a tune, Will." "Stop," Will barks again. A moment's pause, then, "Come on, boy, rise it." Will stares at the floor, surly, pushing his foot against a cigarette butt. "Why wouldn't ye play one?" a woman's voice whines—the only woman on the island bold enough to drink—Maura. A drunk, a negligent mother, worse things I've heard her called. The hated exception that proves the rule. "Just one," she whines again. Will raises the glass he's been dawdling between his knees and gulps down the second half of his pint in one go. "Aright, aright," he mutters, gets up, bangs his glass on the counter, and goes out to a back room to get the melodeon. "Fill that glass for the man, and another of the same for me," a music lover moves in.

Will stalls getting ready, collecting attention like tickets. He's given his drink and raises his glass to the giver—"Sláinte" ("Your health")—a ritual never neglected. At his first note, someone shouts, "That'sh a boy," and someone else shouts something in Irish. Will plays a reel, jerkily, up and down the scale, arhythmical, hitting too many wrong notes to sound authentic, but of course this is authentic. "He's in his cups," Maura giggles—too drunk to play, in other words. But the men lean forward intently, vigorously tapping their feet on the concrete floor—all that's left in them of the urge to dance. The music swings playfully, impish. The men's faces are clenched, hard and red, but their eyes twinkle. Will sways, the music sways with him, that same refrain again, obviously all he can remember or manage at the moment, but no one's tiring of it.

There are places in Ireland where fishermen and farmers play as well as any professionals and are repositories of traditional regional songs unknown elsewhere. This island's musical heritage is battered; apparently the best of the island musicians work in factories in England, only coming home to visit and play during the summer. That's when we'll hear some music, Sean says. Meanwhile, a man with a thin, babyish face stands up, halting Will's next tune, and begins to sing a ballad. It's grief-stricken, plaintive, a love song of farewell with the obligatory beloved Mary, Paddy departing for America—a caterwaul against fate. It could be maudlin, moaned out for the millionth time, but it's not. The song's sung feelingly, as if known firsthand. And in a way it is. All the farewells embedded in this island rise up ghostlike while the young man sings—1,300 people gone since the turn of the century, boats disappearing into the horizon—and from the closed eyes and lifted head of the singer I wouldn't be surprised to see real tears fall and gather on the floor with all the years of tears and spilt beer.

Aside from Sean, the closest friend we've made is named Tommy O'Herne. Tommy is the most educated man on the island, the first and only to get a college degree, a bright spark who made it all the way through university, studying history, then came home to plaudits in order to drink the rest of his life away, his one goal accomplished. It's been ten years or more since that spectacular homecoming—he's in his early thirties—and now his skin's turned purple, his body bony and slack. Just as bad is the slow mental poison eating him inside out, bred of passivity and an unused gift. The gift was substantial—a keenness of mind and superb wit.

Though Tommy's somewhat off-putting in appearance and manner, we gravitated toward him at once, for the talk. And he's clung to us as all the most disappointed have—the bright, betrayed, isolated ones—to have an audience for the talk. He's as opinionated and eccentric as Owen, and their vying banter has become a source of considerable entertainment for the regulars in the pub.

"Well, Owen, did ye ever hear tell of a man in these parts, an Italian he was, and he use'd buy the lobsters one time."

"I didn't."

"Well, he'd had a few hard knocks in his time and he retired out round Clochan way—the Village of

The First Spring

The Skull, did ye ever hear that name put on it, and well named it is too. The night of The Disaster wasn't there forty-two corpses laid out on the quay at Clochan."

"Christ almighty."

"I'm tellin' ye the truth, there was forty-two in it."

"Don't I know you're telling me the truth, and you a scholar."

"Well, now, there are scholars and scholars in it. I wouldn't go comparin' myself to you—"

"What nonsense are you talking?"

"Ah no, Owen, I wouldn't be makin' out that I had all the goods now."

"Give over, will you, and tell your story."

"Shur, yur a great man for the crack, Owen! Well, it was like this . . . I never liked the cut of that man, this Italian, and goin' out one night I had a drink taken, aye, and more than a drink, I had a few drinks on me to tell the truth."

"I bet you had."

"Shur, there was no harm in it."

"Divil the harm."

"Considerin' the day that was in it, ye'd want a few drinks in ye, is the truth, powerful cold it was at that time."

"It's a good job too that we have the drop of whiskey."

"Isn't that what I'm tellin' ye! Many's the night, indeed, I thought that if it wasn't for the bit of whiskey I wouldn't be long for the world."

"Many's the man who thought that too."

"Ye know, Owen . . ."

They never did get back to the Italian.

Tommy has dozens of subjects for talk: island history, island gossip, the state of the country, the rural

62

predicament, the scourge of religion, and, especially, sex. Tommy's life, like Sean's, is mournfully womanless, and he fantasizes continually about the ideal woman who will someday turn up on the island for him, chiding Owen to share me in the meantime. Unfortunately, he grows crude as the evening drags on. All the men who have befriended me are affectionate but reserved; Tommy can't help but take freedoms in his desperation for love.

I fend him off, embarrassed, and turn our conversations to his other uncontrollable aspirations, like money. He always has a new scheme of how we can make our fortunes and stop worrying about money; *we,* Owen and I now in partnership with him—a touching sign of our growing assimilation here. A fish-and-chip shop by the harbor, Tommy insists, would be a winner, what with all the "day-trippers" who'll start arriving in another month on the two cruisers that operate out of Clochan. Owen will fish, he decides. But no conventional fishes—we'll make the tourists eat the odd ones (mockery rising), bottom feeders, eel. I'll do the cooking, naturally. And Tommy will take care of PR, charm them in, spread the word. It couldn't go wrong.

Or we'll get the soapstone industry going, gobs of the stuff back in a West Village cliff just waiting to be taken out and sold. We could even have classes for the tourists in carving. Owen will hack the stuff out. I'll teach. Tommy will spread the word, bring them in.

And so on. The pub rocks with the fantastical. For two hours the idea is real, and details and spin-off plans proliferate. Tommy's reliable for such amusements, always to be found in the same seat at the corner of the pub where the two halves of the bar meet perpendicularly, the center of the universe so to speak, and always to be counted on for a long recap of the day's events, the best of the gossip, or *sotto voce* rumors of a bottle of poteen to be had—illegal firewater from stills in the Connemara mountains.

But some nights, too drunk, he gets contentious and quarrels with other islanders, full of resentment at his own failed superiority. The entire population is material for insults—no one can match him in acerbic eloquence. ("That man would ate his own grandmother, and without salt and pepper either, if he thought it would get him a right of way 'cross Kenny's field.") Tommy's already on probation in Richard's pub for having thrown a dart at a man instead of the board one night, and he's been warned—one more bit of trouble, and out. So when I see him turning surly, I try to draw him back, treading the dangerous line of what he takes for flirtation. "Tommy, you're looking very thin. What did you eat today?" "One boiled egg and a piece of brown bread and three cups of tay, Deba." I scold him, make him promise to take care of himself, flatter him with my concern, and he's momentarily appeased.

Though Tommy and Sean have risen from similar circumstances and are similarly gifted and frustrated, Tommy's turned raucous, malevolent, and self-destructive. Because Sean, on the other hand, is a kind, quiet man, our two friends dislike each other, and neither understands how we could like the other. Sean calls Tommy "a chancer," and Tommy thinks Sean is "too fuckin' tame." They are both compelling men, full of zany, imaginative energy and raw wisdom. Sean lives his life in a necessary bland routine, sharing what he has to give in deeds and stories, and swallowing his despair. Tommy is possessed by longing and spews his despair over everyone in sight; but he does so in a heart-rending way, charged with his articulate intelligence and sense of irony. "Why don't you write it all down," I ventured one drunk night, appalled at the wastefulness of his life.

"Someday, someday," he told me menacingly. "I'll tell ye, when there's no one around to talk to, I talk to this little tape recorder in me room, see. And someday I'm goin' to write a book from it. Me Memoirs, I'll call it. I'll tell it like it is, what this fuckin' miserable life is all about. But there'll be no hero in me book, no, Christ no, because I don't believe in 'em." He spit into the fire. I've never asked him about the book again.

Perhaps naively, I don't believe Tommy will go down the drain—he's too bright and spirited. But Owen is fatalistic about the Tommies of the West of Ireland, the sum effect of puritanism, poverty, and village pressures. Tommy can't, or won't, escape because of his elderly father and the land that's his. But farming's "beneath" him, and he makes his younger brother do all the chores while he spends the afternoons fishing and dreaming and ranting. And every night he gets rotten drunk.

Why couldn't he find a job on the mainland, teach, say, send money home for his father; he's not doing any good at home anyway, only breaking the old man's heart with disappointment. "I'm not able for it anymore, Owen, I'm not able for it."

We have put in a garden, its design a mixture of island practices (thick raised beds, called drills, prepared with seaweed and manure) and the French Intensive Method, gleaned from a book, which makes possible optimum use of our little plot. One corner's full of herbs, including transplanted wild mint from the banks of the stream at Clossy, and wild garlic—sweet and sharp—which grows beside the well. The rest is rows of vegetables to feed us later. Both practical and an emblem of our attachment, this putting in of roots.

I watch Owen read in the evenings long after I've given up and sit musing or knitting, his head rigidly downcast, white hair yellowing from the turf smoke, blue eyes scouring the page. He is rereading for the third time the story of Tristan and Iseult, worrying over it, in part over me, I think. How long will our honeymoon last? He has thrived in his work, has just finished a play, and is devoted to our life together here. I am touched and amazed that this life with me is the one he yearned for during all those heady evenings last winter; how is it, I often wonder, given my inexperience and naiveté, that I am an adequate partner for him? I've been in training, under his tutelage, and we've somehow bloomed together.

Owen is of such a different caliber from anyone I've known that everyone and everything from my past has come to seem inadequate. I saw in him from the start a purity and standard I wanted to define my life with, but now I am disturbingly out of kilter with the only world I'd ever known, cut off, physically and psychically, from family and friends. The few friends who've already come to visit—my girl friends from college—can't fit in, can't make the adjustment to the island rhythm or our impoverished household. Linda is squeamish about the chemical toilet and complains about the late-spring cold. She carelessly dumps waste water into the bucket of fresh drinking water so that Owen must make another trip to the well. She lights the oil lamp at full force instead of letting the globe heat up gradually, so the globe shatters—no reading lamp till we can get to the mainland to replace it. She has no interest in the conversation in the pub, only bemoans the waste of the beaches as we bundle up in sweaters and coats. Owen gets annoyed by her mistakes and lack of enthusiasm, and I find myself guiltily siding with him against her. In my estrangement from her, I see how far I've come, how far into another realm I've already ventured. Owen says I mustn't be sentimental about the loss of my former attachments; I must forge ahead. Walk off the cliff with your eyes open, he says. Throw away your life and wait for it to return on the wind. Just as he has. His courage fortifies me.

It is just we two. We've removed ourselves from a world of peers and are left surrounded by a human landscape that we observe or play off of, but cannot be completely intimate with. So we remain in solitude together with our work and our sense of mission. There is a loneliness and extremity in it that at times terrifies me. In exchange for the richness of the rural, we've given up completely so many things I valued—museums, concerts, films. In my hunger for the screen, I actually snuck into the island inn (which has an electric generator) to watch a film on TV with a couple of early tourists. As I left, I discreetly plucked the day's newspaper from a trash can and spirited it home to luxuriate with by the fire. I'd like to have it both ways. But Owen reminds me that's impossible—money's the issue. And given a choice . . . I choose to stay here.

Robert Bernen, a New Yorker who settled in Donegal, writes:

> People often ask me, both here and elsewhere, why my wife and I chose to settle in Ireland. The question always takes me by surprise, no matter how often I hear it asked. For one thing, what could be more natural than settling in Ireland, given the choice? . . .
>
> But the real answer to the question "Why did we choose Ireland?" is this: I always think it was Ireland that chose us.

Arriving was a spellbound blur, staying has a sense of rightness. For Owen it was a chosen risk, for me a matter of being adrift, overwhelmed, converted. Today out walking I wandered the emptied village of Knock, precipitous on a hillside, its roads overgrown with grass for want of walking. The hardest village to live in, it was the first to be abandoned as the population dropped. The husks of its former houses cling shoulder to shoulder like a line of ghouls. A splendid aisle of rhododendrons flanks the path to the foundation of a house no longer in existence.

The islanders continue to disappear while we, outsiders, appear, resettling the land they've given up on. We feel righteous as we contribute to the island's survival—that's the zeal Harold instilled in us before we even arrived. There are few places where the addition of two could be so significant. But without the islanders, our being here would be meaningless.

The facts of the island speak only of decay, but in the imagination of the people, the island still thrives. Knock is alive, populated. The dead keep pace in the stories of the living.

My writing has opened itself beyond my repetitive inner longings and out to this world of wrenching beauties. The landscape and community play on my imagination. No other place has been as alive for me.

I know I must try to live not as I have up till now, pampered and disconnected from my surround, but in curiosity and harmony with a group of people and the land we share. Bringing me here, Owen has made that possible. I've made my passage official—I've sent my passport to the Garda station in Clifden for my tourist visa to be replaced by a permanent residence stamp. I may remain in Ireland as long as I like, so long as I don't take a job. I'm committed to stay.

Owen has redefined the world for me, and I embrace his definitions as if they were a cure. I take his language and his world view and put them on like a new wardrobe. I accomplish a transformation: jerk my head to the right in greeting on the road, mutter "not a'tall" in the right affronted tone of voice, and call the country I grew up in "the States"—as if it were no longer mine.

The rain hasn't let up. "The wettest May in years!" an islander crows at me. A stranger. Day by day there are fewer strangers. Families have begun to cluster in my mind. Not that anyone is ever introduced—a custom unpracticed here—but walking with Sean, a chance meeting, and if we ask, "Now who was that, Sean?" he'll tell us, and a summary of his foibles as well. "That man doesn't know his arse from his elbow, and a damn pity it is too, for wasn't his elbow needed the other night when Maura's car broke down in front of his house, and him lyin' on the kitchen floor in a stupor." Faces in the pub, names Harold whispers with warnings of who or what not to mention (familial severances and lifelong enemies in a single village—what someone did or didn't say at the mother's deathbed grounds for a grudge that will carry over generations).

Every islander, of course, knows the intimate details of every other islander's life. Most pride themselves on the extent of their knowledge about their neighbors: their illnesses, their temperaments in the privacy of their homes, their eating habits, whether or not they daydream in church, how much they drink, the health of their cattle, how much money they have hidden in mattresses. All 229, by latest count, in a tight, viperish nest, bound only by their having been dropped onto this same outcrop of rock in the middle of the sea. "An island is a terrible place to be born into," Sean intones sometimes when he's drunk. Though they denigrate themselves for their lack of style and success, it is their sense of themselves as islanders, as a separate and superior race, that keeps them going, I think. They fancy themselves more hospitable, more resourceful, more holy, and more courageous than mainlanders. We've already proven ourselves susceptible to that same hubris. It's hard to avoid, perched out here at such a physical remove from the goings-on of the rest of the world, obsessed with our own pressing daily details.

In the midst of the unceasing downpour, the gas ran out on our stove yesterday. I didn't know the warning signs, so now the stove is dead and the island is out of gas; a delivery is due in Clochan in two days. Suddenly life's doubly difficult. The fire must be built up quickly, water put on for tea. At dinner we try to fry a fish, holding the pan over the stuttering flames. We take turns stooping on the floor by the hearth, our legs quickly stiffening. Close to the floor, bent over the fire, I think of the women of these houses a hundred years ago, cold and aching. They at least had a grill to set a pan on, a bunch of hooks at various heights to hang pots from. Many of the houses still have them and some women prefer to cook that way, the tang of turf smoke atavistically half the pleasure of the food.

But this new, unprepared-for difficulty discourages me. I'm hopeless at making a good fire, will never get it hot enough to cook by. And rain falls into the chimney, hissing on the warmish sods. Rain drums on the roof, rain leaks through a spot in the ceiling, plop-plopping into a pot we put below to catch it, rain spreads in under the door till we put a burlap sack across it, the rain's too fiendish to go out in without oil-skins, so we don't, using up the food in store, waiting it out. Inside, damp and cold, we feel like pioneers, grimly virtuous, settling the place in spite of itself.

"How's Deba?" Richard inquires when I finally get out to the pub today in a light downpour—another sign of assimilation, this greeting, what the islanders reserve for their own. When I complain about the weather in response, Richard groans, "The wettest and coldest May I can remember!" "A dirty day"—an old man raises his head sleepily from his pint. "Ah, 'tis only gansey rain today," Richard quickly instigates disagreement, but the man doesn't have the energy to take him up on it. (Gansey rain: light enough that a good gansey—sweater—will keep you dry.) Richard says he'll open the shop for me "after a short while," so I order a cider and wait while more men file in shaking themselves out like dogs, muddy puddles forming on the concrete floor around them. The men strut in their gleaming oilskin suits, cocooned, unperturbed. We still can't afford to buy them. And they're not worn by women. If they must leave the house, the women rush around with their heads tucked in their old black woolen coats like terrified pullets.

"The wettest May in years," Richard reiterates, and Sean, who's just walked in, affirms, "That's for definite shur." (Later it was clear to me that every May's the wettest May in years, and every June and January too, so great is the need to suffer aloud.) Sean's down in the mouth, and when I ask him what's wrong, he says he's "fagged" (exhausted). But it's the rain that's got everyone blue.

"Finish that glass and have another"—Sean buys me a drink to enliven things. "How's the boss?" Richard asks (meaning Owen) as he leans forward and fills my glass. Though that label rubbed me the wrong way at first, it's common lingo, and I don't mind "belonging" to Owen in the public eye, our relationship still being a source of surprise and delight to me. But before I can answer, Michael Hammers cuts in, "He's a smart man to stay away from here," and they all laugh—at me, at Owen, at Richard? "I didn't notice the rain keepin' ye away," Richard retorts. No malice from Michael, though; he's one of the sweetest around. Good-natured kidding is the way to fend off the weather, it doesn't mean a thing—real opinions are mumbled in the dark. Another man pipes up, picking up the thread of the joke, "How smart can he [Owen] be, lettin' the little lady out alone into a place like this?" More laughs, but Sean moves in protectively, not wanting the fun at Owen's or my expense. "Look it," Sean says, "we'd be better off hibernatin' till summer if ye ask me. Ye tell himself he's a smart man and that's for shur. Owen's the man has the headlines [brains]." "He's got a bellyful of books is what he's got." More laughs, a round of Sláintes, and the fragmented breath of our laughter misting the cold room.

Outside, Jack's standing on the quay, staring at the waves breaking over Bishop's Rock. Horses stand on Dooneen, the hillock nearby, staring at Jack. He reads the sea to see if the day is fit for a crossing. The sea addresses him in a language familiar as the one he speaks. What's picturesque to me—flung foam and muscular current—is sign of trouble to him. Every day this week he's walked back up the hill home, leaving the boat to toss and chafe at its chain mooring. The islanders complain that he's fussily methodical, maddeningly cautious. But Jack's a humble man who wouldn't challenge the sea as men do the land. His caution is tribute to the powers that be. There are too many reminders of disasters to ignore. Right there by his feet, the massive red iron anchor from a Spanish Armada ship: it went down off the East Village in an impassable channel between two rocks. Whether all the men drowned or not, no one's sure, but there are no Spanish surnames on the island. The anchor was recovered and brought around to the harbor. It sits just above tideline as a trophy, or reminder, and men always tie their punts up to it after rowing to shore from the big boats.

I toe around the shoreline, treacherous with rocks and a foot-thick bed of seaweed, blighted by plastic and cans. The ruin of the old fish-salting house and the kiln used for years to boil down kelp for iodine, once thriving money-makers, now sit measuring rainfall. Nothing's going on at the harbor.

So I continue on to Rosie's, as every afternoon, to pick up our bottle of milk and return yesterday's empty—a recycled orangeade bottle. Usually the milk is still warm and yellowish waiting for me. Sean is always out, and Rosie and Ann are always in the middle of something, Rosie directing from the fire. The vinyl-clothed table is covered with dishes about to be washed and cooling loaves of bread; basins full of laundry are soaking, a cat's getting into the cupboard and raising shouts, hens are being beaten back from the door. Rosie and Ann, though ostensibly busy, in fact waste most of their time. If they're not gossiping with a neighbor, Rosie is usually gazing into the fire muttering to herself, and Ann's gazing out the back window toward the harbor looking for a topic of conversation. One day I came on her peering out the window through binoculars. Embarrassed, she shoved them under some papers on the windowsill, but went on to mention several minutes later that the boat was coming in and there were "strangers" on it.

Today Ann was out when I arrived, and Rosie had evidently been awaiting me anxiously. It was only the second time I'd been alone with her, and the first since we had failed to go to church on Sunday morning. She hobbled over to pour the milk and took her time wiping around the cap with a piece of muslin.

"So ye don't go to mass then . . ." She couldn't look at me.

Her state of anxiety prompted me to come clean at once. "No. I'm not Catholic."

"Oh? . . . Aye . . ." She pushed things around on the table and knocked over a jug of cream. "And yur husband?" It seems Sean, out of timidity, has succeeded in shielding his mother from the fact of our marriage-lessness.

"Well, Owen was raised a Catholic, but he doesn't go to mass anymore."

"Tch-tch . . . well . . ." It was apparent that the latter was easier to take than my admission. "Well, what religion are ye then?" she forced herself to ask while working a rag over the spilled cream. "Protestant?" The word pained her.

"No . . ."

"No?" Her head jerked up. What else was there but Catholic and Protestant? Except for Africans and Chinese—heathens—which I obviously wasn't . . .

"I'm Jewish."

"Aye?" she shrieked. She reeled and made the sign of the cross in the air near me. "There never . . . never was one of yur people on this island before!" she stammered. "There was a Russian here once though . . ."

"Really?"

"Aye . . ." She wiped off the milk bottle for the third time and shook her head slowly, muttering. The idea that a Jew was standing in her kitchen was proba-bly too ludicrous to believe and I did, after all, seem a decent enough person. She suddenly turned to me and smiled sympathetically. "I suppose there's no church of yurs in these parts . . ."

"Church? No . . ." I told her that it wasn't terribly important for me to go to church, that simply leading a virtuous life counted for a lot.

She squinted at me, baffled. This was a religion beyond her comprehension. I stood paralyzed waiting for an axe to fall, for the island to be snatched from me. Staring at the fire, her mind worked away, and gradually she seemed to decide that I was really as religious as she was—what she wanted to believe from the start—though in a mysterious way. She smiled and slowly nodded her head at me. "Well, yur a great girl to come all this way where there's no church of yur own a'tall." She handed over the milk bottle, stumbled back to the fire, and meekly said good-bye, embarrassed by her transgression of curiosity, but not unpleased with its result.

I stepped out with relief and walking home, happy in the downpour, remembered Djuna Barnes's curious equation: "The Jew and the Irish, the one moving upward and the other down, often meet, spade to spade, in the same acre."

There is a tiny wiry man, retarded, who boards with the eighty-year-old postmistress. It's said Mrs. O'Malley more or less adopted him from out of a mainland institution; he's known as Seaneen Post Office (Little Sean of the Post Office) in contrast to Sean the Post, the actual postman. Surnames are never used in these two instances. Seaneen helps the postmistress out around the house now since her husband died. He is incessantly good-humored—that unwavering cheerfulness of the not quite comprehending. I often meet him on the road, and he repeats whatever is said to him in greeting, broadly smiling.

The First Spring

"Great day."

"Great day, a great day, it's a great day."

"But there may be rain later."

"Rain, rain . . . there may be rain later, ah, rain."

"Well, good luck."

"Good luck, good luck then."

He seems perfectly harmless but apparently he does something peculiar every few months or so, like letting the hens loose in the night, or draining the water tank for no reason.

Mrs. O'Malley is an island institution. She's had the post office for over fifty years, is known to listen in on telephone conversations and peer inquisitively through envelopes. Business is conducted in whispers through a narrow slit in a sliding wooden window. She moves at the lumbering pace of a tired old tortoise, broad and heavy, and always wears a dark wool dress with a huge brooch on her bosom. Grey hairs sprout from a mole on her cheek. Her head pops in and out of the window slit, but her body stays firmly in the shell of "the office."

I have come both to dread and cherish the business of mailing. I dread it because I must allow at least an hour for the ritual. But once I'm in the presence of Mrs. O'Malley, I feel oddly excited.

There's always a line at the post office. Because the business of communications is so personal, one waits in the porch appended to the actual office until the person ahead is finished. "Ye'd be destroyed waitin'," the women complain. The post office has the island's only public telephone. Mrs. O'Malley writes the number one wants on a government form and retires to her switchboard console, out of sight of the window slit. One can hear her though, pounding on the board, trying to get the attention of the operator on the mainland. "Hello

Clifden, hello? . . . Hello . . . Hello Cleeefden, are ye alive or dead over theres? Can ye hear me? Aright. Hello? Aright then. A trunk call. IBF-101. Hello? Hello! Aye. 11:14, Code 17, 682-294. Right, right ye are . . . They're gettin' it for ye now." The latter to the fidgety caller. How long will the tenuous connection survive?

The telephone is notoriously unreliable; it breaks down for days at a time leaving us incommunicado with the world, or sometimes temporarily dies in the middle of a conversation. At best, it crackles and undulates—a thing of the sea. There's angry talk in the pub some nights about demanding a second telephone line from the government, a backup system (all five telephones are in fact extensions on a single cable—an intimately shared party line). Some say "the second line" is already a certainty. Others declare it will never happen—"They wouldn't give us a thing, the robbers."

After an agonizing wait, Mrs. O'Malley shouts, "They have it for ye now. Go on. Go on!" The caller rushes around the corner to the "call box," a kind of a booth designed to provide privacy, but which, rather, amplifies the caller's private business for the edification of the rest of the office.

"Hello? Is that Mr. Mannion? Well, ye sent me the wrong shoes. I asked for a girl's size three and you sent a four, and they're useless to the poor girleen . . . that's right so. What's wrong with Janie a'tall? She did . . . is that the truth? God bless her . . . I will so, but I expect to be credited for the postage and the call. Well, now how was I to know ye'd understand it if I just posted them? . . . Right so. Good luck then."

The caller comes out and returns to the window wiping her brow. Mrs. O'Malley is always sure to hang up the telephone in time to be at the window when the caller returns. The only time I've heard her move fast.

"That's 15p."

The First Spring

"I'll want to be postin' these shoes now."

Shuffling from the waiters in the porch. This will be a long one.

Mrs. O'Malley disappears with the package and we can hear the weights of the scale being dropped, picked up, tested. She lumbers back. "I'll have to check the book," crooning good will. But ominous. Which book? In which drawer? Minutes pass. Books full of obsolete postal charges, in the old money, are consulted and discarded. A cardboard poster is taken down from the wall and studied. "There's no parcels on this one." More books, fine-print footnotes. "Is this a parcel or a packet, would ye say?" (A distinction I've yet to comprehend.) "Because if ye'd call it a small packet . . ." "It's a packet, I'd say." "Oh, then . . . well I suppose that'd be 38p." "38p? Good Lord!" "It's right here, see—" She proffers a mottled scrap of government type. "It's not that I was questionin' ye, Mrs. O'Malley, but the prices of things!" "Sure they're goin' up faster than ye could count. Desperate." Mrs. O'Malley searches through several folders containing the various denominations of stamps that might add up to thirty-eight. When she's finally assembled them, she spits onto the back of her hand and rubs the stamps across the spittle, then pastes them onto the "packet" haphazardly, angles all askew. Then she tosses the packet to the floor to be dealt with later. The first time I saw Mrs. O'Malley apply stamps in this fashion, she reddened in embarrassment and explained that if she had to lick stamps all day, she'd be poisoned by now. A sponge device provided by the government sits dryly on the windowsill.

The shoe-packet woman then leans forward to the window slit and whispers. I can just make out her request, "a pot of strawberry jam," and am filled with despair. Mrs. O'Malley keeps a limited number of groceries behind her counter, and some people make a habit of buying a few things after their calls and postings. It's said poor Mrs. O'Malley doesn't make much from the post office, and it's a kindness, as well as a convenience, to buy a thing or two from her. I haven't developed this habit because of how long it takes Mrs. O'Malley to walk across the room, find the item, return with it, then ask if there's anything else.

"A drum of salt," the woman whispers. Mrs. O'Malley sets off across the office again. She returns a few minutes later. "I'm all out. Sorry now." Sighs. "What are those biscuits there?" "There?" "No, to the left!" "Here?" "No, those above. Those with the red on 'em. Those." "Oh, these. They're somethin' with nuts in 'em." "Nuts? Oh never mind, so. I wouldn't ate anything with nuts in it."

Mrs. O'Malley waddles back to add up the bill. I can hear her reciting the list of purchases as she writes them down and realize she's forgotten to include the phone call. The woman doesn't correct her. This is why Mrs. O'Malley doesn't do so well from the post office. But I've found that Mrs. O'Malley overcharges as often as she undercharges and the two tend to average out, so I've never risked correcting her mathematics either.

The woman puts her jar of jam in a string bag and smiles apologetically as she leaves. My turn. "Oh, it's ye . . . ye . . ." Mrs. O'Malley gurgles having lost my name. "Well, how're ye gettin' on up there? A windy spot, I'll tell ye. I remember when Jimmy was alive and livin' in that house of yurs, God rest 'im, the stories he'd tell about rain pourin' into the kitchen, God help ye, pots full of it. That's the God's honest truth. I wouldn't understand a person livin' on that hill, things is bad enough down here, the Lord knows." The last on an inhale, adding poignancy. I assure her we're doing fine, so far, and she gazes at me in stupefaction. "Well, I wish ye lots of luck, lots of good luck."

The First Spring

I buy as many stamps as I can afford so I won't have to repeat this task too soon again. But as I watch Mrs. O'Malley search her black folders for the seven-penny stamps, I begin to feel that odd excitement. I'm on tiptoe leaning over the wooden partition watching her broad fingers rifle the drawers. Everything she touches exudes the thick perfume of turf smoke because of a bad chimney which draws more smoke in than out. The telephone rings and Mrs. O'Malley has to go to the switchboard to answer it. I study the dusty shelves with the groceries, the big grey canvas bags on the floor the mail goes in and out in. The call's for the guest house. "There'll be visitors agin in no time," she mutters coming back, "and every one of 'em wantin' to send a post-card home. Desperate." She resumes her search for stamps. She flings around her black folders, mangling papers in the drawers, and she almost upsets the little cardboard collection box just inside the window slit soliciting contributions for a holy shrine to be built somewhere in Mayo at the site of a considerable miracle. "Here ye are now." She counts the stamps out again to make sure she's given me thirty, trying to show a little professionalism for my sake. I lean in, looking at her old wooden till and the jar of pennies to one side as she counts out the wrong change for me. And though some-one else is waiting in the porch, I don't want to leave now. I want to linger at this hub of the island, try to win Mrs. O'Malley's confidence and hear some of the gossip she's renowned for spreading. So I ask for a pack-age of the nut biscuits ("Oh, ye like that kind!"), and as she walks over I shove my head in the window slit and get my first good look at the ancient switchboard con-sole, a tangle of frayed wires. She returns and I pay up. "Good luck then," she giggles in farewell, and the phrase momentarily takes on, after her talk about our house, the American connotation of "You'll need it," so that I can't suppress a shiver.

The nut biscuits were damp, of course, and soured with turf smoke.

This morning, like an attack, shattering the silent grey sky, the sound of aircraft. We ran out, terrified, to see a helicopter passing over the island. Astonishing, one helicopter, such a massive intrusion. Where had it come from, why was it here? When we lowered our eyes from the sky, we saw that everyone in the village was outside their front doors, eyes fixed above. I rushed across the road to Theresa.

"Where did it come from?" I demanded of her, hungry for facts as is still my American wont. "Is there an army base nearby on the mainland? A search going on? Was one ever here before?"

"America . . ." she muttered wondrously. "It's come from America."

"But . . . I don't mean . . ." I was disoriented, agog.

"America," she whispered again as she walked back into her house wagging her head side to side, and the small helicopter chopped off toward the western horizon, over that flat table of sea in the direction of my country.

My country! The dream they'd all escape to if they could. My country which I think of less and less as I replace it with this one, this island world and the nation it's nominally attached to, this troubled Ireland. Every day on the radio, I listen to the catalogue of unbearable details from "the North" as if they were mine to grieve over.

The North looms invisibly above us; I see a map in my mind's eye on which the North is colored blood-red, though on official maps of the world it's colored the same as Britain and set off from Ireland which is usually colored green. "I have four green fields," the song goes, referring to Ireland's traditional four provinces, "but one of them's in bondage."

It is easy and obvious to say that the British don't belong in Northern Ireland and that internment without trial is barbarous. But exposed to the reality of this war, even secondhand, it's harder to espouse radical solutions than it is from afar. When the radio reports the killing of a British soldier or two and someone in the pub shouts "Good man" in celebration of the killer, I am as disturbed as when the radio broadcasts a British minister blithely saying that Northern Ireland has, for the moment, "an acceptable level of violence." Irish support of the nationalist cause often blurs judgment of its means. That so many apparently gentle and intelligent people I've met don't seem more disturbed by the violence of the IRA surprises me. But given the historical context, I shouldn't be surprised. By now their response is inbred, automatic, the result of centuries of rancour and defeat. The idealistic zeal with which they embrace even minor issues is symptomatic of the general temperament of a people long shoved to the edge, always ready to assume offense, always ready to take a stand.

Talk in the pub is often passionate: "We'll never rest till all Ireland's free"; and "It's a sin." But only the shedding of Catholic blood is a sin for the men at the pub, and the IRA are the same immortal men of balladry continuing their march to martyrdom stanza to stanza. Cuchulain and Fergus, Brian Boru, Cathleen Ní

Houlihan, and The Easter Rising remain planted on the horizon mythologizing daily life, giving form to anger and hope. The islanders have no concept, really, of nail bombs, snipers, or gelignite, have never seen, even on television, body parts collected in plastic bags. They rotely stand by a drummed-in national ethic, proud of the men who freed them of Britain, proud of the men who continue the effort in the North. Richard is the only man I've heard speak against the IRA. He's also the only islander who reads the papers. Everyone else, including Owen, is only waiting for an excuse to launch into a tirade against the British.

Groping for my own opinions about the problems of the North has begun to replace my former political concerns. Most of my friends are still marching against the Vietnam War and the presence of Dow Chemical recruiters on campus. They all think my coming to the island an admirable move. It doesn't seem to matter that I've abandoned the central arena of the times. I, after all, have seemingly allied myself with one of the world's great political victims.

But I can't claim that as my motivation. Have I motivations at all, or only vague instincts and the willingness to try to jolt myself into further consciousness? In some ways, given my preoccupations, I think it's the language of this new home—a new language within my own—that has most affected me.

As it happens, ours is one of the few islands of this coast that speaks English as its first (and only) language as a result of political circumstances not unrelated to the current strife in the North. Up and down the coastline are some of the last strongholds of the Irish language, communities protected by mountains or treacherous water that have held out against centuries of infiltration. Because of the fine harbor visible beneath my window, this island, despite its seeming isolation, has, in fact, been at the center of the coastline's traffic for God knows how long, stopped at, invaded, fought from, fought over, influenced. It had a prison on it during the Cromwellian invasion, and one can still hear Elizabethan idiom frozen into the island's English from that first, brutal exposure. Some of the Englishmen from that period stayed—they're present still in family names like Schofield (spelling and pronunciation altered to Scuffuld), Ward, and King. Later the French came by and left behind Lavelles and D'Arcys. In the nineteenth century, the English built a barracks on the island, and the English language stuck. But, as elsewhere, the adoption was ambivalent.

The islanders took English and transmuted it into their own subversive, spunky language. They refused certain letters outright—*w*, it seemed to them, was a strange letter to start a word with so they turned it into *f*—"the *f*ind is blowin'," they say, and "the *f*ite cow." *W* was reserved for the rare *v* in the logic of Irish grammar which loves to shuffle consonants—"*w*ery bad" after drinking "*w*odka." Vowels went altogether haywire, closeted between strong consonants. One-syllable words became two-syllable words: *f*ar-um (for "warm"), co-old. And to confuse the matter (and the master) further, they speeded it all up to 78rpm and refused to open their mouths more than a quarter of an inch. This rapid-fire rhythmic mumbling which veers and sallies up and down the scale has insinuated itself into my mind and taken grip. Its melodiousness and syncopation makes even a conversation about laundry a pleasure. It's a way of talking, in fact, that's designed to create and take pleasure, so it could not fail to delight me, just as its intimacy delights me—"Now, Deba, I'll tell ye what it is . . ."

They've fought back against the English in the only way they could, in the conquerer's own tongue,

though even their syntax anticipates denial: "Ye wouldn't
throw a sod on that fire, would ye?" they cautiously request. They've come to love the power of language, both
its power to tell the truth and to delude. They know
well its tricky surface. This folk story always makes me
think of them: There's a witch, who like other mortals
will die if stabbed; but if stabbed a second or third or
fourth time, her charm saves her. So when attacked on
the road, the witch cries out in mock surrender, "Pull
the knife and stick it again!" inspiring her attacker to
a frenzy and thus ensuring her survival. In a similar way,
the islanders use language to fend off outsiders. I heard
Sean with an early tourist who was full of questions, a
man who'd come to fish but had been confining himself
to the island lake where there are reputed to be tench.
No one was sure—a fish hadn't been caught there in
years—but one islander said a Frenchman caught a
tench there, ten or twelve years ago he believed, by making bread balls and soaking them in absinthe. The tourist immediately rang Clifden to import a bottle, and
had spent his days lakeside, without success, since. He
was thinking of trying the sea. "How do you know how
to get safely into the harbor?" the tourist queried. Sean
pointed to the three white towers strategically aligned
between harbor and hill and explained how when you
line them up from the sea you are assured safe passage between the castle and Bishop's Rock. "How do you know
if there's enough water at the quay to float the big boat?"
the tourist asked. Sean pointed to the signal rock. "How
do you know in fog how close you are to land?" the
tourist continued. Sean was fed up with the cross-
examination so shot back, "A bee in the mast is a very
bad sign." The pub roared as the tourist puzzled. Sean
sat back with his invented proverb, smug as a Buddha.

The play of language especially manifests itself
in naming. Every protruding rock and curve in the road

has a name in this miniature world in which hills are mountains and streams rivers. And nicknames abound. Tony Coon Mara, Tony the Sea Urchin, is what a man with coke-bottle glasses is called, the look of his eyes having once reminded someone of those globular shellfish. A particularly gossipy old woman is known as Radio Brazzaville in tribute to that widely broadcasting African station.

Le mot juste has taken up residence on the island tongue. My own speech seems anemic in comparison, too slow to rise to the occasion, not worth the effort it takes an islander to decipher. So I am humbled. The iambic underbeat, capricious pitch and syntax of their sentences lulls me, shorts out my own spoken and written rhythms, just as inexorably as Owen, up to now, has shorted out my opinions and approaches. And I wonder how much my falling in love with him, as my falling in love with the island and the Irish cause, depended on this enchanting bombardment of words.

A whale lifts its back out of the sea and anchors itself somewhere. Drawn by gales, rocks and seaweed gather on it and eventually bushes begin to grow there. Sailing ships that happen to be passing take it to be an island and land. The men make themselves a fire to cook a meal. But the whale, when it feels the heat of the fire, plunges back into the sea, pulling the men and their boats down with it.

So fire is still the best test for an island, because fire is the enemy of every sort of phantom. And a fisherman, when he sees an unfamiliar island, will still row up to it and empty his pipe out onto the soil. If it's a fairy island, fire will make it real and solid, and he may land. And if it's a whale and goes under, he will have saved himself a lot of trouble.

Owen has developed an obsession about scavenging for firewood to supplement the meager turf we're managing to beg, borrow, or buy. Not a tree grows on the island, but he comes home with armfuls of wood—dead twigs of bushes found in ditches, bits of crates, scraps from a barn under repair, and best of all, what's washed up from the sea. Whole telephone poles and ships' masts appear, the prey of storms, the memorabilia of wreckage. They wash up in coves, at the foot of cliffs, or on beaches exposed to the prevailing wind and current. There are some real gems, and we're by no means the only ones interested in them. As Pat Mullen says of the Aran Islanders, and it seems to be true in general of islanders and coast-dwellers, "All of them are crazy after driftwood, or in fact wreckage of any sort." However, few of the islanders would burn what they scavenged, as we do—they use it for fenceposts and repairs.

There are rigorous unwritten laws about driftwood gathering which Owen has dutifully absorbed. The wood belongs to the man who plucks it from the sea or wrack and moves it above the tideline. There he can leave it without fear, to be washed by rainwater and dried by wind and sun, bringing a donkey and cart to collect it at his leisure. The inviolability of ownership is sacred, except for one variable—time. Vague and subjective as this consideration is, if a man has left his wood sitting for too bloody long, it's up for grabs again. How long is too long? Weeks, months, a year? Such distinctions lie in the mind of the man who wants the wood; and on a predawn mission there's no one around with whom to argue the point.

Owen hasn't yet dared such a secondhand claim, though Sean is egging him on. I say, if Sean thinks it's the right time to pounce on those three gorgeous logs under Knock Point before someone else does, and he's sure Paddy never wanted them in the first place but just claimed them because he nearly fell over them one morning, well then let him go along on the expedition and take half the bounty—a log and a half. Owen agrees this would be a reasonable precaution, given our tenuous standing in the community, and has proposed it. Sean says he doesn't mind going, but "What in the hell would I be wantin' with any of that wood?"

Today when I went to get the milk, Ann did not disguise her binoculars. She squinted out the window at the incoming boat to confirm her first impression. "The Doctor's on board," she shouted, excited.

'Oooohh . . .'' Rosie crooned.

The Doctor. I have never seen this doctor, only heard of the rarity of his appearances. There is only a nurse resident on the island (Catherine Walsh, wife of the pubman Richard); every Thursday the doctor is supposed to come in and hold a clinic at the tiny prefab building that was deposited by the government beside the harbor. But his trips are highly irregular, any day of the week at all, maybe weeks between them, at the whim of the weather and his own mysterious schedule, and if one doesn't live within binocular view of the harbor, how to know that he's come at all and get to the clinic in time? Rabid word-of-mouth's the operative mode. Anyone moving on the road is messenger. "The Doctor's cumin' in"—a woman scurries by. Farther up the road, "The Doctor's *in!*"

The rush starts. Old women limping down the long hill to the harbor. Wan children dragged by the hand. Ann puts on bright red lipstick in the bedroom and tightens her kerchief knot under her chin. I walk out with her. The roads are busy. Can all these people be sick? We see Sean cutting across a field and ask him if he's going to the doctor too? "Naa, I'm goin' to have a pint." But from the hill we see him go past the pub toward the clinic and Ann chuckles malignantly.

Most people look reasonably healthy, but complain vociferously of mistreatment at the hands of the nurse and errant doctor. All deaths are blamed on one or the other of them. I've even heard it suggested that the doctor's a drug addict, only coming in to replenish his supply from the island's stockpile. Others are content to call him alcoholic.

One neighbor, Eileen, recites the illnesses of her family whenever we meet, and berates the medical establishment, such as it is, bitterly. Woeful tales of missing the doctor, a bad cold getting worse, then three weeks later, by the time he came in again, pneumonia. She herself has problems with her feet and frequently complains, "Anything with the feet is a terrible hardship." Later, in reference to her husband's poor eyesight, she modifies, "Anything with the eyes is a terrible hardship." She throws her head back, eyes to the sky, and inhales on a sigh, an artist of complaint.

Problems give Eileen's life meaning. The mantel is lined with pills, potions, and ointments. The children, dirty and underdressed, run amuck. "A *slew* of children," Tommy describes them. "They was always heavy breeders in that family." The oldest child, a ten-year-old girl, is carrying the gurgling baby around on her hip. The second eldest turns up, feet dragging in oversized wellingtons, having drawn a kettleful of water from the well. Two younger children are drawing on the wall with crayons. Another one's running around in the rain with only a thin shirt on. "Get back in here out of the rain and put a jumper on," Eileen yells out to him. To me: "Is it any wonder with weather like this that they're down with the flus all winter and summer too." The child yells back, " 'Tis only dry rain." "Is that why it's makin' drops then?" "They're only dry drops." The child runs out of earshot.

Almost yearly, Eileen's taken out on the deck of the boat and ferried to Galway in the rust-eaten van that serves as ambulance to give birth at the regional hospital. Delivery practices there are routinely risky. For convenience, most births are induced, the women heavily drugged. Once, at the height of a winter storm, Eileen went into labor and the boat couldn't budge. So Catherine, who's a qualified midwife, delivered the child up in the house just as children were always delivered here. Eileen was not pleased. Each new affliction is a badge of honor for her—proof of her rotten lot.

Today she heads triumphantly across the village with three of her children reluctantly in tow. She trundles them along with an air of mission, nervous, pious; she mutters that she has a "stomach complaint."

The nurse that Eileen and the others love to insult is also the island innkeeper, and a rather extraordinary woman. Distracted and tense, Catherine usually manages three conversations at once—two in the kitchen and one in shouts on the intolerable telephone (vibrations of Atlantic flux warping syllables) ordering supplies for the inn. The sick line up and the soup simmers and pie dough covers the counter top that also serves as examination table.

The First Spring

Catherine's raised five children, been sole proprietress, for all intents and purposes, of the island's health for thirty years, and expanded the inn, which dominates the harbor area and which she runs almost singlehandedly, to twenty-six rooms (wouldn't I agree it has to be called a hotel now, she queried me). The health care of the citizenry often gets squeezed between more pressing daily problems, like getting some potatoes dug for dinner and finishing reservation letters in time for the mail boat. Except for births and genuine emergencies, she tends to feel put out by sick calls. "There's not a thing wrong with any of those women," she gripes to me as a cluster approach the back door. She gropes for her glasses, hung from a chain around her neck, to confirm who they are.

How healthy are they? On an island with no birth control available, where women produce babies in rapid succession with little prenatal or postnatal care and with primitive hygiene, where the womb of more than one woman has simply burst after the fifth or sixth child in as many years, where a miscarriage is called a "miss" as if it were merely an inconvenience, a missed beat . . . even the hardiest of them suffer. And given their inadequate diets, poor sanitation, and the cold, they're afflicted with endless flus and infections. But Catherine also deals with a high percentage of hypochondriacs, people for whom illness or imagined illness is at least an occasion. Ennui sends them knocking on the hotel door.

Catherine is the only woman, aside from old Mrs. O'Malley, who is addressed by her married name—Walsh—rather than her maiden name. This is because she's an "outsider," a Boar Islander who's only been here thirty years. Local women are known by their maiden names for life except for letters and official business. Less a feminist gesture, that, than a sign of the importance of family lines. Catherine, of a non-island family, stands apart.

She also stands apart because she and Richard are the only bona fide money-makers on the island. Given their ownership of the pub, shop, and hotel, and Catherine's position as nurse, they come second only to the priest in power. Their decisions shape island life. Because they are reasonably well off, there is the inevitable mix of admiration and resentment of them. No one's willing to regard himself or herself as less clever, so they suspect Catherine and Richard of trickery. They discredit the inheritance of the land the pub's on, scowl about county council connections which supported the hotel expansion, and so on. But Catherine and Richard were once poor too, and are tireless workers. Catherine was the eldest in a large family and took over at age eleven when her mother died in childbirth at twenty-nine. She was educated on Boar Island only through grammar school, but got herself over to England to study, then practice, nursing. She came back to marry Richard Walsh, but immediately went off to take a year-long course in midwifery so she could qualify to become district nurse. Her success is a matter of extraordinary energy and ambition. For whatever reasons, ninety-nine percent of the islanders lack that. "She's a hard woman," Richard marvels.

The fact of Catherine's education is another insurmountable obstacle between her and the island women. She and Tommy are quiet allies in that regard. And, like Tommy, she was interested in us from the start, though suspicious. Why had we come, the usual question. And what was Rosie giving us or not giving us. And why hadn't we been buying meat from her (i.e., what the hell were we eating). But we soon earned her affection because almost as much as Tommy she loves to talk, especially to outsiders. She is starved for stories of life abroad, for news of cities, and craves our opinion of events and trends. In return, she treats us to reminiscences of the scores of interesting visitors, many literary, who have shared her roof, and gives us plenty of practical advice and lore, including local folk medicine (which she tries to practice, but is thwarted in by the islanders who demand pills as proof of modern medical care). With her range of experience, intelligence, humor, and verve, Catherine's the most eloquent woman on the island.

The price of conducting a conversation with her, though, is constant interruption. She's never in one place for longer than five minutes. Tasks or duties are abandoned for the suddenly more pressing; if a catch of fish comes in that has to be inspected, the house call waits (thus her tarnished reputation as nurse). During the time we've managed to spend together, though, I've grown very fond of her.

I often go down to her kitchen in the late afternoon to chat and drink tea. It is a jolt of modernity. The hotel and the priest's house are the two places on the island that have electricity—a private generator in Catherine's yard rumbles on at nightfall and mealtimes. The generator makes possible a host of modern appliances, but not quite enough for the amount of work that goes on in that kitchen under the glare of a row of fluorescent lights and the gaze of half a dozen madonnas. While Catherine scurries around, I laze, drinking her Boar-style tea, boiled black as coffee, eating homemade scones and butter, and listening in on the theatricality of her life, so diametrically different from our own here.

"Darling, tell me, what am I going to do about this darn oven? Richard, is that Richard? Where's the milk a'tall? I haven't a drop of cream for the dinner! Who's that? *Who?* Oh, tell her I've no bacon left. Not a rasher. Sorry dear. I haven't a clue. I must call Clifden

. . . Sorry Debbie darling, I . . . Oh, I'd say that bread is done . . . What is it Richard? The bacon, is it? I really must, you know . . . Debbie, dear, would you ever pick up the phone, that's a good girl, and ask for Clifden 33 while I—you're very good, pet. Dear God, the bottoms of these loaves is burned again. Richard, something's got to be done about this oven. I can't be— Richard? Oh darn. Why ever does this . . . who's that? What's the matter, darling? Your finger is it? Come here till you show it to me now like a good boy."

I haven't yet been sick and had to wait between potatoes and trifles to be seen to by the nurse, but it seems to me Catherine's kitchen is a more appealing place to go to the doctor than any I've known, and her unusual fusion of the modern and old-fashioned is an attractive rarity. While peeling twenty pounds of potatoes a minute in her electric peeling machine, Catherine can still take pleasure in remembering the early days of her marriage when they didn't even have running water. Often on a Saturday when the children were young, she says, they'd pack a picnic lunch, row across the harbor to a little lake behind the castle, set up a portable gas heater, and do the washing and bathing outside. The kids were plunked right down into the lake along with the rinsing diapers and sheets. Wet clothes were spread out on the rocks to dry while they picnicked, and they wouldn't go home till dusk. Just twenty years ago. "I'd say, you know, that we had much more fun those days," she says. "Maybe we were even happier."

By now we have sorted out the web of stories surrounding that castle built into a cliff at the tip of the harbor.

The First Spring

It was apparently built by a Spanish pirate by name of Don Bosco in the mid-sixteenth century. Wisely, he allied himself with his contemporary, the infamous Irish piratess of this coast, fiery Grania Uaile—in English Grace O'Malley—who, from this castle and others, terrorized shipping up and down the coast.

Richard lent us a punt to make a pilgrimage. Most tourists, apparently, end up making foolish spectacles of themselves when they walk out to the castle at low tide across the narrow channel that separates it from the harbor's arm, then get trapped out there when the tide comes in. "By rights there should be some kind of a sign up warnin' them"—Richard is uncharacteristically social-minded. His merciless ribbing of the tourists is legendary. That Richard is denying himself the possibility of this pleasure by lending us his boat is heart-warming.

Just through the Spanish arch entrance of the castle is a large central courtyard with the remains of a well in it. Around it, rooms build outward and upward, many-layered, labyrinthine. Though decayed, the castle is still starkly beautiful, sturdy and broad, its stone merging with the cliff it's precipitously built into at the end of the peninsula. Water rushes up at it while slits in the walls keep watch. Big windows tower over foaming rocks below. On the castle's floor of nettles lies centuries of litter.

Don Bosco is said to have buried a heap of treasure here before he died and put it under spell so it could never be exhumed. Once when a priest tried to dig it up, it's said he was ordered to stop by a voice speaking in Irish from underground.

Most of the castle's early stories dwell on the pirate queen Grania Uaile, an extraordinary woman who battled and cajoled her way into secure power while men were executed left and right in continual strife with the English. Born in 1530 into the O'Malley clan, which owned the island from 1380 until 1873 (*Terra Marique Potens*—Powerful by Land and Sea— was the family motto), she spent her girlhood on the water and knew the coast inside out. She also knew what the politics of survival were—the right marriages, the right divorces, the right alliances—building for herself a huge domain and becoming Ireland's sole female chieftain. These wild, isolated waters bred in her an unmatched gutsiness.

She spent her time on the sea controlling the traffic of her territory in a thirty-oar galley. She and Don Bosco kept their fleets in this harbor behind a chain strung across its mouth. From the strategic perch of the castle, she kept watch. And, no doubt, from those round windows cannon were shot and many a man flung. Foreign ships were guided up and down the coast, for a fee, and "she supplemented her income by engaging in the more lucrative but dangerous occupation of piracy, which was also a highly competitive business along the west coast. That she was successful in this is beyond doubt. . . ." Sir Henry Sidney (father of poet Philip, who also met Grania, and was said to be captivated by her) reported to Queen Elizabeth of his tours here: "There came to me also a most famous feminine sea captain called Grany Imallye. . . . She brought with her her husband for she was as well by sea as by land well more than Mrs. Mate with him. . . . This was a notorious woman in all the coasts of Ireland." "She seemed well used to power," a poem commemorates, "as one that hath dominion over men of savage mood." Certainly she had dominion over her husbands. And legend has it that when in the heat of battle once she saw one of her sons lose courage and shelter behind her, she shouted contemptuously, "Is it trying to hide behind my backside you are—the place you came from?"

The First Spring

For years, Grania's cunning alliances and charm kept her out of trouble while the English fought the chieftains for control of Ireland. She was condescendingly treated more as a curiosity than a serious threat, a bias which she turned to advantage. But finally she was arrested, and her unwomanliness condemned. Lord Justice Drury advised the Queen: "Grany O'Mayle, a woman that hath impudently passed the part of womanhood and been a great spoiler, and chief commander and director of thieves and murderers at sea to spoille this province, having been apprehended by the Earle of Desmond this last year, his Lordship hath now sent her to Lymrick where she remains in safe keeping."

Grania, however, somehow extricated herself from safe keeping in Limerick, and then brilliantly, fearlessly, decided to face Queen Elizabeth herself and bargain some security for her old age. She sailed through war-fouled waters to England and talked her way to an audience with the Queen, some say barefoot, some barechested, but certainly in regalia never before seen at court—she was the only Gaelic woman ever to reach that chamber.

Most endearing about this meeting is that Grania seems to have regarded Elizabeth as her equal—Queen of Connaught calling on Queen of England. But in fact she was savvy and probably humble in mien because she was coming not only for pardon but for financial assurances. Legends abound. How delicious it is to imagine these two powerful, drastically different women face to face. But what's certain is that Elizabeth was touched, despite all those letters over the years from her governors describing the treachery of Grania Uaile. In fact, more bluntly, Elizabeth was duped by the wild Irish piratess, for Grania's every wish was granted in the end, much to the dismay of Sir Richard Bingham, Grania's archenemy, who did his best to deny her what the

The First Spring

Queen had generously, naively, ordered. The Queen directed Bingham thus:

> And further, for the pity to be had of this aged woman, having not by the custom of the Irish any title to any livelihood or position or portion of her two husbands' lands, now being a widow; and yet her sons enjoying their father's lands, we require you to deal with her sons in our name to yield to her some maintenance for her living the rest of her old years. . . . And this we do write in her favour as she showeth herself dutiful, although she hath in former times lived out of order. . . . She hath confessed the same with assured promises by oath to continue most dutiful, with offer, after her aforesaid manner, that she will fight in our quarrel with all the world.

Grania fighting in alliance with the British? Bingham knew better. The other clans were offended at even the promise. But principled patriotism was irrelevant for Grania—a realist, she bought her safety once again and lived out her life as she pleased, plundering and conniving, becoming a vivid symbol of Irish grit and wiliness, the subject of numerous songs and poems—"No braver seamen took a deck in hurricane or squalls/Since Grace O'Malley battered down old Currath Castle's walls." Too old to fight finally, she would appear on deck in a white nightgown, her hair flying, and scatter foes who thought her a ghost.

Big feisty women here are nicknamed Grania, in honor of her rare example of womanly authority. And her continued mute presence in the walls of the island castle is a constant anthem to woman that probably helps the local balance of power.

It's intriguing to imagine what the islanders were like in Grania's time, their harbor controlled by pirates, their boats impounded. Probably they were just as spunky, rambunctious, and hard as she was, being fish of the same water. And I can see the remnants of that century still in the island character—all their craftiness and bravura, the toil of survival taken in stride. But the castle's history didn't stop with Grania Uaile, nor the island's character-shaping.

After the deaths of Grania and Don Bosco, the castle fell into disuse, but in 1652 was taken over by Cromwell's invading army and turned into a barracks— that strife with the English unending. As MacGiollar-náth says in his history, "In the long night of the seventeenth and eighteenth centuries all Connemara was a prison into which dispossessed refugees were driven." Not only refugees of religious persecution, but all sorts of outlaws roamed the valleys and heights until Connemara became known for its hospitality to the lawless and homeless and was flavored by those it welcomed. It was also flavored by the tyrannies it witnessed. Priests were hunted like animals in the mountains. By 1656, the Island of the White Cow was a penal settlement for captured priests who were shipped in from all over Ireland. For some it was a stopping point before deportation to the West Indies. For others it was the end of the line.

Just across the mouth of the harbor from the castle is a treacherous half-tide rock called "Bishop's Rock." It pops up out of nowhere when full-tide waters start to fall. By low tide, its stark peak is a sentinel and grisly reminder. The most prestigious prisoner the soldiers got their hands on was the refugee Bishop of Clonfert. Barbados was too good for him. So was the bleak prison they'd fashioned for grave offenders out on the island's north shore on a strip of rock called "The Hag's Causeway," a band of red dolerite on which it's said a spell was cast so that men lose their way on dark nights and are never seen again. So many prisoners were slaughtered there that nearby fields are still reputed to be dyed red with their blood.

The Bishop was rowed out to the rock now named for him at low tide and bound to it naked. Then the English soldiers returned to the castle to watch the slow, steady rise of the tide, taunting as it reached his chest, then his chin, until the Bishop was wholly submerged, drowned. The daily baring and swallowing up of Bishop's Rock is a chilling living memorial.

And so the English were here, and brought their language and terror and a few of their genes to island life. But the island survived the invasion, the character of Grania Uaile prevailed—the islanders talked back and managed, for the most part, to live as they pleased. Do they still? It's clear that the younger islanders lack that edge, that degree of spunk, wiliness, and resourcefulness that I prize in Sean and Catherine and Bridget. It takes pride to fight for one's home, and that pride is on the wane. Those like Tommy, exposed to the outer world, see little to be proud of in the island so turn their strength against themselves. It could be we are witnessing the end of an era that's lasted centuries, a way of life and character handed down unaltered for as far back as one can trace, now gone soft. The current invasion of the modern might be more devastating than Cromwell's.

The island in lush, noisy, nearly summer glory. An explosion of wild flowers. Larks erupting, plummeting, erupting again. Fat bees like helicopters. Donkeys in perennial conversation across impassable bog and crag, crying out in futile desire—long-drawn-out hee-haws left to echo in the empty air, then contagiously taken up by others. P.J. and James converse in a field, P.J. bent over his spade, James in his perpetually bent posture—two low figures against a blueing sky. The sea relaxes.

There's tremendous energy abroad these long days, work in the fields and bogs whenever it's dry, late nights drinking, no time to sleep, daylight making everyone drunk for life. On the other hand, Richard says that in the winter the islanders hibernate during the long nights and hardly show their faces in the day. So life's lived closer to the realities of the season, animallike.

How stirring the midnights are as we approach the summer solstice and the sun finally, after eleven, dips just below the horizon and draws itself east, barely out of sight, a thin strip of white light crossing the northern skyline for three hours till sunrise again. "The light passing the north," Synge called it. The sun glares into our window by four, bright silence keeping the mind astir.

Tonight, out walking alone in the glassy midnight dusk, I look at the island as for the first time again, reliving my thrill in arriving. My head dizzies with the beautiful calm. I think I know now why I've been willing to alter my life so radically. Life has become vivid to me as it never was before. It's as if everything I've done up to now has been a step removed from reality, veiled. A bank of machines stood between me and experience. What did clean clothes ever mean? Now when I boil water, soak, scrub, wring, and hang out my clothes to dry, I feel I have washed clothes! Likewise, light is not a switch, but lamps to fill with oil, a flame to ignite. Weather asserts itself, defines the day. All the casual facts of life have been dissected, discovered, made real for me. Because everything is foreign, laid bare, I am forced to rethink and feel it as if for the first time.

The First Spring

That's why I'll learn to be a better writer here. Ordinary life is true experience as it never was for me in the States. Far more than a new language or a new vista, this is an initiation into the stuff lives are made of.

Tonight, the long finger of the harbor is rippling silver, pointing. The huge "Stags," great wrinkled rocks that trail off from the island's northwest corner, are like a stage set pasted to the sky. The rest of the landscape slowly sinks and fades, islands dissolving into mist, back to their first enchanted state. Vivid tang of salt, doors to houses flung open, teapots and plates of bread on kitchen tables, grey specks of houses still visible on the far green hills of the mainland, and before me the chimney of our house, smoking, Owen waiting beside the hearth.

Summer

In Ireland, for a few years more, we have a popular imagination that is fiery, and magnificent, and tender; so that those of us who wish to write start with a chance that is not given to writers in places where the springtime of the local life has been forgotten, and the harvest is a memory only. . . .
—John Millington Synge, Preface to *Playboy of the Western World,* 1907

It poured last night, Saint John's Eve, the summer solstice, so there were no bonfires on the islands and mountains as is the still-practiced pagan custom. The twigs Sean and Owen gathered all week for the ritual today revert to ordinary kindling.

"A soft day," a man calls out to us as we walk back from the shore to the house. Drizzly, in other words. Not soft like the balmy Junes of my childhood. I miss those seamless days, but it will soon be July, and Sean promises things should improve—"June is a month that can go either way, if ye know what I mean," he says.

We've been out "picking winkles," a demeaning task for islanders, for us the pleasure of free food. Periwinkles are all over the rocky shore after high tide and one can quickly gather dozens. Winkles, in the old days, were one of the few ways of making money—an exporter bought them to ship to France where the islanders imagine they're a delicacy. He paid four pounds a hundredweight, a pittance considering the long cold work—they weigh only a few grams each. The price has gone up a bit in recent years, and Sean says there are still a few who will do it. He might even consider it himself if things don't improve. But no islanders eat winkles themselves—the postfamine shellfish stigma.

The same goes for certain fishes. Michael Hammers came up the other day, shouted outside the door, then stood back gazing at the sea. In his hand, two fingers slipped through the gills, he held a big grey fish. "Well, ye's have a great view up here, I have to say that."

"We do indeed."

"Because there's not much else to be said for this spot," he laughed. East Village snobbery—the Middle Village is disdained for its exposure and its numerous ruins. We waited while he took his time, elongating the pleasure of his mission." "Would ye's ate that fish?" He held the creature forth.

"Why not?" Owen theatrically arrogant.

Michael mocked, "Well, there's no one on this island'd ate that fish."

"Why not?"

"Because it's a dirty fish, a cousin to the catfish."

"Still, it might be very tasty. What's its name?"

"I don't know its proper name, mind ye, but we call it the Franach. And there's a brother to it, a kind of a sort of a dogfish we call the Fragach. They do get caught in the nets, a terrible bother altogether. Sometimes this German fellow comes round from Connemara and he'll buy the Fragach, but no one'll touch the Franach."

"So why are you bringing it to me?"

"If ye don't want it . . ." Michael chuckled and made to fling it into the field for the waiting gulls.

But Owen grabbed it from him. "What are you doing to that lovely fish?"

Michael gave it over, guffawing. "Sean said to me

ye'd ate anything, and he was right, shur enough. Good luck to ye's then."

Owen brought the fish inside, humiliated, but determined to enjoy it. So we've acquired a reputation as people desperate enough to eat anything . . . well all right then.

But, not surprisingly, the Franach was delicious, a delightful light, lemonish flavor, and thick, firm meat. So we sent out word that we'd take any Franach caught, and it's now become a source of great amusement on the quay. Tommy was impressed and said maybe he'd taste it sometime, and why don't we name that fish-and-chip shop we're going to open "The Franach and the Fragach" . . . ah, yes.

Our reputation has been further complicated, or perhaps tinged is the word, by our association with the island's single greatest outcast, a broken man derisively called "The Flame." Unwashed, scabrous, only a smudge of bright red hair vitiating his self-imposed darkness, The Flame is the only person on the island (excepting Harold and ourselves) who doesn't attend mass. He's a vociferous atheist—ungraced, how could he believe in the grace of God?—and virtually a hermit, a blight on the island fringe, greedy, childish, tactless. He hates everyone but us.

Hardly the sort of man I'd usually want anything to do with. But Owen is perversely attracted, curious, perhaps for the same odd reasons The Flame's attracted to us—as fellow outsiders. The Flame ingratiated himself with us by offering us land to grow potatoes on, our garden plot being inadequate for more than a smattering of vegetables. Ironically, he's got one of the biggest and richest fields on the island, the envy of his devout neighbors. And so Owen and he have formed a kind of partnership, helping each other plant and tend in exchange for our use of the land.

Tommy ribs us about it endlessly. He finds our choice of friends other than himself offensive. "Well, had The Flame any interesting news from inner space for ye's today? Ye'd want to be careful, Owen, because they say it's catchin', ye know." Catherine marvels, though, saying Owen's had a great influence on The Flame, and that he's a saint to even talk to him.

A step beyond The Flame, which even Owen has not braved, is his younger sister, known as Baby Chop (origin uncertain). She rushes about the island blindly babbling to herself, colliding with whoever's foolish enough to get in her way. She even, The Flame informs us with malice, eats on the run, not having sat down for a meal in decades. The two of them live completely separately at the two ends of one house, Baby Chop refusing to cook for her brother because "he hasn't the appetite of a thrush anyways." At least twenty cats are the beneficiaries of her cuisine, however, clustered outside the door at her end of the house beneath a canopy of rags she's erected in the bushes. The Flame's end is curtainless, wrecked. We sometimes see him at night through the bare window sitting bent at the edge of his sagged bed eating corned beef out of a tin can, his sunken eyes staring into the wall—a staggering portrait of loneliness.

Finally the rain has let up and it begins to resemble summer—cool but fair. Still, big clouds come and go, exposing then taking the light, recoloring the landscape. The weather forecast runs one of two ways: cloudy with bright spells, or bright with cloudy spells. There's no noticeable difference between the two.

However, the dry weather has sent the population out to the bogs and fields in gusts of activity. It's already late for turf cutting—only a couple of months left for the sods to dry before they must be hauled home for winter—so men are spending whole days in the bogs cutting and stacking. Owen's gone to work with Sean in exchange for a stack of turf of our own for next winter. I'm to play the customary role by bringing them sandwiches, tea, and cake at midday. The bog is far and inaccessible, over a big hill at the northeast corner of the island. I set off in the footsteps of centuries of lunch-bearing women over the stone-littered and boulder-strewn fields, climbing over the remains of stone walls that divide the seemingly useless terrain, and walking through swamps of osiers and sallyrods that baskets are made from. The outraged screeches of pillabeens bombard me as I intrude on their territory. The birds are as aggrieved and self-protective as the villagers they survey from above.

Owen and Sean, gritty with turf dust, rejoice at the arrival of the picnic basket and fling their spades to the ground in welcome. Together we eat on a high rock perched over acres of shovel-sculpted bog, a deep brown moonscape, specks of men working in the distance, the cries of sheep shifting ground. Owen and I are dreamy, Sean intimate and affectionate, but Sean won't linger after his second cup of tea and hurries Owen back to turf cutting—good working days can't be allowed to slip away into gazing talk.

After helping them stack the turf in little three-sod piles for drying, I head to the hotel where I've promised to do some paper work for Catherine. On the way, I see dozens of men inspecting the progress of the hay or working in potato fields, clearing weeds, reshaping the drills after all the rain. Whiskey bottles, full of the morning's milk, are propped up against walls waiting to refresh them. Jim-John passes me on the road with his empty sack on the way to his field.

The hotel is in high gear, the tide of tourists about to change from trickle to flood. I type letters for Catherine in the middle of her frantic kitchen, the phone ringing with inquiries, bread overheating in the troublesome oven, stacks of fresh-washed sheets waiting to be folded, gallons of milk to be separated, butter to churn, supplies arriving on the boat with crucial things missing and unwanted things substituted so that she must change the menus accordingly and asks me why couldn't she make Turkey Tetrazzini with chicken anyway?

A pair of tinkers, Ireland's gypsies, turn up to huckster pots and blankets—commercial products, not their own handiwork as in the past. Catherine hems and haws over the goods, asking for details, but then declines to buy anything. She and the other island women who drift in are secretly excited, but won't let it show— tinkers are at the bottom of the class ladder and give them the rare opportunity to be snobs. The tinkers borrow a donkey and cart from Richard and go off to tour the island door to door. Once they're gone, Catherine sniggers about the time a tinker fell in the well and no one would draw water from it for a month. Of today's visitors she mocks, "Their hair is so wavy, you'd get seasick just looking at them!"

The influx of tourists into the hotel is, for me, already a disturbing invasion. The harbor area's gone international: Dublin accents, English accents, Dutch and German and French. Mrs. O'Malley huffs in exasperated confusion under the onslaught of the postcard-mailing crew. When I go in to buy stamps, she peers suspiciously through her slit, then flings back the panel when she hears my voice, giggling in relief, "Oh, I thought at first ye was one of the hikers!" There's discomfort in the pub: those who refuse to cooperate and go off into corners to drink alone or with a buddy, and others, like Tommy, reveling in the diversion of the invasion.

For Tommy, it's a chance to be heard, and also a chance to be bought drinks. He nightly attaches himself to a suitable-looking couple and regales them with island tales for the evening while the pints keep getting filled. Richard can barely contain his disdain as he fills Tommy's big glass again. Tommy, babbling away in his inimitable fashion, spots us and winks. He pontificates, gives the tourists what they want to hear: "The so'east wind is a very dirty wind in these parts. There's a story told here about the loss of the *Maisie,* a fine hooker, sailin' out on a Sunday mornin' from Westport with a load of flour in her and a breeze from the south. Now the men skipped mass that mornin' in order to go with the full tide and that was their first mistake that day, though they say when a man's time has come, no good sense in the world will keep him from his death. So anyways, they sailed out, but when the tide turned and started to ebb, the wind backed to the so'east and freshened. They should've waited till after the tide turned, ye see, to find what the wind would do, the weather always changes with the tide. Well, the day turned to a gale and a burst of hailstones let loose at them till they couldn't see past the bow of the boat a'tall and the wind blew them straight onto the rocks there off the East Village where ye's was walkin' today and they were all lost, the lot of them." We listen in, it's a new story for us, and we're as impressed as the tourists Tommy's busy charming. We can't help but wonder how much Tommy's initial friendship with us was, like this, a form of prostitution for the sake of alcohol.

For us the pub's gotten tedious, too predictable a pattern ruling it, too much tension in the air. Regulars walk in with a mixture of curiosity and dread. We are snobbish and stick with our clique of friends, avoiding the tourists. But in general the islanders are bound by their sense of hospitality and are welcoming to strangers no matter what. They'll interrupt their own conversations to accommodate them. Outside, they'll stop work in a field or come out of the barn to comment on the view. Understandably, they have a natural hunger for outside contact and a desire to see their lives through the eyes of others. To the more sensitive, however, this is a dangerous enterprise—the eyes of outsiders are full of stereotypes and only passing interest.

Some islanders show their distaste for the tourists in subtle, humorous ways, as in the following conversation between a jaunty Dublin man and one of the few working island fishermen:

Tourist: "Tell me, Paddy, what would you do if you were out in your boat and a big storm suddenly blew up?"

Paddy: "I'd throw anchor, give 'er rope, and wait it out."

Tourist: "And what if the wind got worse, Paddy?"

Paddy: "I'd give 'er more rope."

Tourist: "What if it got even worse, Paddy?"

Paddy: "I'd give 'er more rope."

Tourist: "Paddy, what if the wind was the worst you ever saw?"

Paddy: "I'd give 'er more rope."

Tourist: "Where did you get all the rope?"

Paddy: "Where'd ye get all the wind?"

The tourist slunk away and the island men, laughing quietly, raised their glasses to Paddy.

We've begun to appreciate how protected we are from these disturbing confrontations because of our hill—few tourists will climb it. When they climb the short steep hill just behind the hotel to get to the low road, and are faced with a right turn, a left turn, or a long steep hill, they invariably turn right or left. So we seldom see a sudden flash of unfamiliar colors or hear an explosion of loud foreign voices. The hill is now a divide between two worlds. Yet we are often drawn down it.

After a day of solitude, the verbal glitter of the pub is sometimes irresistible. It is the only center, the only place the constricted voice of the island rises into play and song, shucking discontent. I never think of the compulsive drinking that goes on in the pub as alcoholism. The ferocity of pub life is the ferocity of loneliness. Drink is the ticket of admission and the emollient of discourse. The stories it oils are the necessary gestures of a people watching the fabric of their lives disintegrate around them.

The first true summer day, a brilliant Sunday. We shelved all work for the day, packed a lunch, and took off for the west end of the island while everyone else was at mass. Beyond the West Village and the last outpost of human life, the landscape alters into a wilderness of crag held up by cliffs. Seabirds gust close overhead and hundreds of rabbits flee into burrowed slopes, alarmed at the human incursion. We walk among droppings and bones, relics of the bog, stumps and skeletons, a dead day-old lamb with its eyes plucked out by birds. But for the screeching of the offended, patrolling birds and the grievous cries of sheep, we could be in the dead remains of a blasted world. The islanders seldom come here. They never walk for pleasure. They walk to shop, to get to the bog, to visit one another, to find stray horses and cows, to look for driftwood. But not out here on the far lonely worthless western edge which bears the brunt of the Atlantic's mayhem and where the only thing to do is to meditate on the stark beauty—for me an ascent beyond the human, an inspiration.

On an isolated peninsula we found a sun-warmed rock pool and, deciding to swim, giddily began to undress. But Owen suddenly stopped in trepidation. Trepidation because he felt we were about to commit a grave offense against island ethics by skinny-dipping. The community would not tolerate such an affront to its morals, he was convinced, and were we discovered, we'd be kicked out. By the priest? I asked incredulously. By a committee specially formed for the purpose? Very simple, he said—no one would rent to us.

Owen always insists, and the evidence seems to support him, that the islanders are rigidly asexual—though I heard a teenage girl say of her brother and a group of young women tourists who'd been in for the weekend, "I think John had one of those girls last night." Raw and harsh, that "had," those encounters.

I was ready to break loose, run riot, but with the paranoia Owen had generated, it was hard to feel very Dionysian; still, the water was gorgeous and the sun exhilarating after the cold wet spring. I teased him, pulling him under, but he struggled away, said I was "daft," and looked around anxiously for spies. That just made me tease him more: I climbed on his shoulders, bearing my breasts to the island sky, and hooted till he threw me off and got out. I finally got out too, dried off in the sun, and dressed. We idled over our picnic and wondered about how different life might be here, given sunshine. Maybe it's all that clenching against the cold and wind that shapes the island psyche, more than the Church and economics.

At the same moment we both became aware of a loud noise, an engine, coming nearer. Terror gripped us. We'd been spotted, they were coming. Already I felt dismally responsible for having drawn attention to us with my shouting.

A car trundled across the bog. It was Maura's. It came up to us and stopped. Will, the melodeonist, stepped out along with a professor from Dublin we'd just gotten to know who was renting a house nearby for the summer. They walked forward solemnly. The Dublinman spoke: "I've been sent as plenipotentiary."

"By whom?" Owen trembled.

"The island."

The Dublinman paused.

Owen's voice cracked. He was stricken. "Yes?"

"The Boars have landed."

"The . . . they've what?"

"And challenged us to a match."

Owen began to breathe again. "A match?"

"We bate them last summer," Will chimed in, "and they're goin' to play dirty for shur."

"Will you ref the match?" the Dublinman pleaded, terrified by visions of revenge.

Owen was laughing now. An invasion of Boars had challenged the White Cows to a match. It was mythic. It had nothing to do with us. Owen said of course he'd ref it. "Yur a credit"—Will landed a hand on his back. They squeezed us into the back seat of the car.

Owen had played football (Gaelic football, a cousin of soccer) for his county, and when we arrived, the islanders had known his name for that rather than for his writing, which had touched him. Now they were looking for him to control their rivals, ensure their victory. "How'd you know where to find us anyway?" Owen finally mustered the courage to ask.

Will: "Ye were seen headin' west by John Cloherty's wife—she's too old to be goin' to mass anymore. What were ye doin' out among them useless rocks anyways?"

"Taking pleasure in the fine day," Owen smug now.

The car bolted over the shingle beach between the Lake of the White Cow and the North Bay—a crescent of stones thrown up out of the sea, mesmerizing to walk on, ridiculous to drive over. A field full of bleached rocks turned to a field of sheep rushing away at the noisy approach of the car.

The Boars' boats were tied up off the East Village. They were a wild-looking bunch all right—torn T-shirts, crenelated haircuts, missing teeth, and ungovernable eyes. Only men. Women avoid boats except for the rare essential trip to the mainland for childbirth or shopping. Sun sharks had followed the boats into the bay and now playfully leapt in the bright light—a sign, Sean said, that summer will soon settle. Off all the islands of this coast, the shark was once hunted for the oil in its liver, but the skill to harpoon died out with the advent of paraffin, and now the shark connotes only good weather.

The East Village was welcoming the Boars warmly, every man, woman, and child out in the carnival atmosphere. Tales of the winter, how they'd gotten through, who'd been sick, whose barn was damaged in the January storm. Unfamiliar names.

Sean headed to the field with us to survey the terrain that would serve as the "pitch"—well, a kind of a pitch, a rabbit-burrow-strewn expanse more or less level, the sea lapping one end of it, sandy and soft. Too soft to play on? "Divil the bother," Sean shouted gleefully, bubbling with eventfulness.

He told us there are sixteen families on the Island

of the Boar, and fourteen of them are named O'Toole. How do they keep track of themselves, I asked, then I wondered about inbreeding and the wild look in the eyes of the Boar men. Sean said they use their fathers' and even grandfathers' names to keep themselves straight—Jim-Michael-Paddy O'Toole, John-Jack-Stephen O'Toole, etc. Catherine is an O'Toole. And the actor Peter O'Toole believes his ancestors came from Boar Island and has built a house outside Clochan with a view of it.

Our team assembled, rather ragged-looking themselves. Big grins on their faces though, already tasting victory. One Boar protested that Owen was as good as a White Cow by now, and there'd be no justice in the reffing. Our team drowned him out saying Owen was not, and what's more, never would be, then winked at Owen as they took their places on the field. They all crossed themselves and waited for the whistle.

An explosion of feet, running, kicking, impossible to keep track of where the ball was, the quickest game I've ever seen, but Owen always on top of it, agile as the young players, running with a whistle clenched between his teeth. He was nervous, I could tell, with the ferocity of the playing, and steeled himself to call a foul against the Boars. They accepted it sullenly and took off again. More violent kicking, Owen dodging boots, and the Cows scored a goal! Cheers and shouts from our side-lines—more islanders than I'd yet seen in one place—"Glory on ye!" "God Bless the Cow!" No time lost, they were at it again. But suddenly Owen was looking around in confusion and the play was disintegrating amidst angry shouts.

"The Cows is playin' ten men," the biggest of the Boars screamed down at Owen, "and there was supposed to be nine in it!" (Nine was the agreement, fifteen the usual team number.) Owen lined them up and officially counted. Boars: nine. Cows: ten. It was true.

He looked imploringly at the Cows. "Shur there's no harm"—Will came forward. "Leo said he wasn't playin' so Brendan took his place and then Leo came in the end and forgot to tell Brendan . . ."

"What kind of a ref is it anyways?" the big Boar spat, then, "Come on men." He began to lead them off the field. "We came south to play football, and we've been swindled instead." They were stomping off.

"*Stop*," Owen shouted with sudden authority, and they turned. He waved them back. A huddle now, inaudible negotiations. Once the Boars started off the field again and had their own huddle, then returned. After fifteen minutes, with no announcement of the decision, but with Brendan leaving the field, play resumed fiercer than ever. The Boars scored a goal and were fiery with vindication. Then the leading edge flip-flopped between the two sides, a tight game, but after another half hour of play, the Cows edged the Boars out by two points and were declared the winners. A tinged victory, but a victory nevertheless, and the Boars weren't mean about it. In fact, now that they'd played out their ritual, everyone was relaxed, slapping each others' shoulders and quickly heading for the pub. We followed, Owen near nervous collapse.

I flattered him for his stamina and authority, how he'd managed both to keep up with the boys and to keep the peace. And I kidded him about his terror in the bog—by then he could laugh about it too. All his brash rebelliousness crumbling over a rock pool!

The Boars were all gab when we got to the pub, and one offered a toast, "We're glad to be among ye's." The big Boar came forward then and formally asked Owen if he'd ref the return match. What return match? The next good Sunday, the Cows would travel to Boar Island to play, and would Owen ref it again seeing as what a good job he'd done? So Owen was vindicated too, and another toast went up, "To the return match," Owen's voice the loudest in the room.

An old man from Boar who'd come along to watch said to no one in particular, "Shur, this'll never be forgot, never be forgot."

Voices on the radio in professionally bleak tones: "Four armed and masked men . . . the victim shot eleven times in the head and chest."

A government crackdown on the IRA here in the Republic since last month's big breakout at Mountjoy Prison. Cabinet ministers who were tried and acquitted of gunrunning for the IRA (though most still assume them guilty) now piously lecture us on the successful suppression of terrorism. Change the vocabulary—Fenians, freedom fighters, terrorists—and you can say anything. The ambivalence of the Irish politician faced with the modern IRA is profound. A republic just over fifty years free, made free by the IRA, must now as a matter of policy and decency condemn the progeny of its liberators. The obligatory speeches of condemnation after killings and bombings are often bitterly laughable—defensive, hyperbolic, insincere. The fathers and grandfathers of these so-called murderers are national heroes.

There's tension in the pub these nights when the news comes on the radio as there are often English tourists present. Most don't dare open their mouths about politics and sit with heads bowed during the recitation of deaths and political maneuvers. But sometimes the more devilish islanders will try to goad them with mumbled remarks of the "terrible conditions" in the North.

One foolish Englishman bit the bait, lost his temper, and warned how the violence would spread—even to here—and attacked the use of children as terrorists in "Londonderry." The room curdled to silence. It's not surprising that linguistic distinctions should be so politically loaded in this eloquent country. Anyone who says official "Londonderry" rather than the long-used Irish name "Derry" reveals by that two-syllable choice his ancestry, religion, politics—his entire being as far as the Irishman is concerned. I've learned to tremble at these violations of the code. I saw Owen become furious as the Englishman resumed his uninformed harangue, madder than I'd ever seen him, a terrifying, atavistic rage. "Patronizing bastard," he spat. I was shocked at how much under his skin the Englishman was able to get, how a certain type of imperiousness automatically triggers fury in the Irish. The roots of the tragedy of the North became all too clear. The foolish Englishman left the island the next morning.

And another one arrived to take his place, this one descending from out of the skies in a privately hired helicopter and landing on the village commonage just behind The Flame's fields; birds, cows, and sheep scattered in terror to create a clearing for it. And out the gentleman came with cane and monocle to inspect the place. Flashback of landlords. Island-hopping. Twenty-minute glimpse within a hundred yards of the expensive waiting chopper. The islanders, drawn out of their houses by the noise, watch from a distance, bemused, bothered. It is so easy to suffer again and again the un-healing wound of colonialism.

The island has only been free of a landlord for fifty years. A 1914 report to the Congested Districts Board (which eventually bought the island from its last landlord), written by Douglas Hyde et al. at the suggestion of patriot **Roger Casement**, described the island's houses:

> House fourteen feet by twelve. Two chairs.
> One rough table. A cow in the corner. Behind
> the cow a space boarded off, twelve feet by
> three feet. A large rock, forming back of fire-
> place, also shut off a little chamber with bed.
> Three or four straw crosses (St. Brigid's
> crosses), and a couple of holy pictures; two
> doors, dungpit at one of them. Six persons liv-
> ing in this house. Four acres of land, bog and
> rocks. Rent 32/- a year.

> House twelve feet by twelve feet. Floor,
> living rock, natural drainage hole in middle.
> One door; pig in room. Bed fills up one end of
> room. A half-starved pet kitten. . . . Herme-
> tically-sealed window six-inches square. No
> land. No fence around house. Bedding con-
> sists of sacks filled with straw.

Tourism reopens the wound. The islanders' only resis-
tance has been to refuse to sell the houses or sites they
finally own to outsiders. For years, tourists begged and
offered dreamy prices, but the islanders wouldn't yield
their land. But this year, a few have succumbed—the
financial need and allure finally too great.

Tommy ridicules the lack of pride and principle
in those who have sold out. But he, of course, sells out
nightly. Now, as if in retribution, he's finally been
banned from the harbor pub as Richard's been threatening for years. A real knock-down, drag-out fight the
other night between Tommy and an East Villager. Ostensibly nothing to do with tourists and the history of
landlords, but those tensions are so much in the air
these days that it's hard not to see it in that context. Dis-

possessed, purposeless Tommy, on display on his beautiful rotting island.

So now he's banned, for life, from the pub at the center of island society and forced to the dark pub in the far west for all his drinking and gossiping and performing—an internal exile.

A wisdom tooth just cut through the surface of my gum got stuck and infected. The infection quickly spread into my ear and throbbed terribly. I went down to Catherine to discover that the nearest dentist is sixty miles away in Galway. Islands are great places, I thought, as long as you're healthy. However, a Dublin dentist, Dr. Manchester, comes down to Clifden every weekend to his holiday home there, and on Saturday mornings pulls teeth between ten and noon. Luckily it was Friday, so I'd only to wait one more day. She told me to look for him at O'Leary's pub.

We had to hire Jack to make a special run to Clochan for us as the boat recently stopped making the Saturday mail run in a new government cutback. He would wait for us while we went to Clifden and then take us back in.

Clifden has a charming, alpine atmosphere, ringed by the twelve mountains we watch from the island. It has two perpendicular blocks of pastel Georgian storefronts behind which squat a couple dozen small, musty shops. There are two churches, four hotels, and a library which opens three hours a day except on Thursdays. After months on the island, Clifden feels like a bustling metropolis. We'd have to come some Fair day, Richard had insisted, to see the Connemara ponies and the folks in from the mountains. That's an event. There are plenty of mountainy people in all the time, though, slow gawkers unfamiliar with money, compulsively browsing even as they pay for sheep-worming powders, fertilizers, rope, meat. We're rather wide-eyed ourselves.

I found O'Leary's pub and joined the line of sullen men and whimpering children at the bar. The dentist's office was in a storage room at the back of the pub furnished with dozens of empty Guinness barrels, stacks of six-packs, a tattered armchair, a coal stove on which a pot of simmering water held the official instruments, and Dr. Manchester, attended by his wife and a white toy poodle. I sat down terrified in the armchair.

With hardly a question I was given a shot of Novocain. It had no effect, so he gave me another and I was sent back out to the bar to wait for it to take while he pulled someone else's tooth. I still had almost complete sensation on returning, so begged for a third shot, after which Dr. Manchester commenced to struggle with the short exposed piece of my wisdom tooth while his wife held down my trembling head and the poodle jumped into my lap, panting. Minutes seemed to pass with no give; when the tooth was finally yanked free, all four of us sighed. He washed off the troublesome tooth, offered it to me as souvenir, and said to take some aspirin when I got home. I had a stiff drink at the bar first—Mr. O'Leary and Dr. Manchester have a lucrative Saturday morning practice going here.

The pain of the infection soon returned worse than before. Shivering and dizzy, I staggered off the boat into Catherine's, then home with a bottle of painkillers, and went to bed for two days, full of self-pity for the conditions I was suffering under—my first brush with illness here. This week I've been taking it easy and am spending a couple of hours a day with Rosie learning how to knit the "Aran" designs.

At one time, the design of a fisherman's sweater helped identify his home village in case of drowning. Now the patterns are arbitrarily mixed, and Rosie knows them all—she even won a national knitting competition some years back. Rosie is not so good at explaining her talent though, and our conversation sweetly wanders while I clumsily tackle popcorn stitches and double diamonds. Rosie intermittently seizes the needles to show me again, a little impatient and bemused by my lack of skill.

Theresa heard about my lessons and stopped me in the road to send a message to Rosie. Our acquaintance with Theresa has steadily warmed. She even had a cup of tea with us one morning after running in the door unannounced to shout that a sheet of mine had flown off the clothesline. "Quick, quick, come out to it, and we'll catch it before it flies to the north bog itself." We've never been in Theresa's house. It's surrounded by a stone wall about three and a half feet high in which no space for a gate was left. Theresa flings herself over the wall on arriving home and disappears behind a hedge of veronica. One evening, I carefully scaled the wall to bring her a gift of fresh mackerel—we'd gotten several on the quay. I knocked at the front door and could hear her mumbling and moving inside, but she didn't answer. I knocked again and called to her. Louder mumbling, but still no move to open the door. I was perplexed. Just then, Jim-John passed and sized up the situation. "Just leave it on the windowsill there, daughter," he said. I did as he instructed, though worried about prowling cats, and climbed back out over the wall. When I was safely on the road beside him, he shouted, "Theresa, take yur fish!" Then quickly to me, "Now go on home ye, hurry up. Good night, good night now."

Not much hope of getting to know her better, it

seemed. But then several days later as I passed the house on my way to Bridget's with my big shopping basket over my shoulder, she jumped out of the bushes and gasped, "Are ye goin' over, child?"

"Uh . . . I'm going to the shop in the East Village."

"It's over yur goin' so." (I've since discovered that "over" equals East and "back" West.) "Ye'll buy me a two-kilo bag of wholemeal. There." She slapped an old plastic bag at me with a fifty-pence piece tied up inside it, and started to flee. Then she sprang back and grabbed my arm. "Only the Odlum's is what I want. Shur Richard's shop is hopeless. God love ye now, go on."

Now she trusts me for errands and messages and we sometimes chat. She and Rosie are old pals, but don't see each other any more as Rosie can't get to mass. "The crature," Theresa whispered affectionately (creature, a term of endearment). I asked her why didn't she go back and visit Rosie once in a while herself.

"Oh God help us, astór (treasure), I don't be walkin' anymore," she said, though she's up and down the hill all day.

"How long is it since you've been back West?" I asked her.

"Oh thirteen or fourteen years or so."

"You mean you haven't been to the West Village in all that time?"

"Oh no, daughter, I don't be walkin' anymore."

"How about the East Village, how long is it since you were there?"

"Oh, the same I'd say, thirteen or fourteen years or so."

I gripped myself. "Theresa, how long is it since you've been to the mainland?"

"Oooohh, now, I'd say it was twenty-five years

125

since I was last in Clifden. There was no cars in it a'tall at that time and no word about them either. Shur, the world's turned round entirely."

She took off down the hill to the well.

Harold came by with prophecies of doom. He is depressed and broke and worried about the Common Market. The Irish populace assented to membership on January first. Harold's heard reports that the price of butter will rise to fifty pence a pound, that our most plentiful products will become hard to get, and who cares if French wines will be widely available—who can afford them anyway? There will be a large sales tax added on to everything, including food, which will go straight to the EEC. It will hit people like us hard, perhaps make it impossible to live on the economic fringe as we have here. Harold's enraged. The population, of course, loved the idea of psychological approbation by "Europe," little Ireland in league with the giants, part of "the Continent." The government says membership will stimulate the economy, bring Ireland into the twentieth century. But most fear it will just raise prices to twentieth-century levels, and little else.

Harold's a worrymonger, and righteously dogmatic too, so this is just the kind of bad news he needs to set him off into a brooding fit. His work hasn't sold well, he's run out of funds, and now he's trying to get on the dole, which he defensively insists he's as entitled to as anyone else on the island. It will be a psychological setback for him though, not earning his living as a painter. Whatever little he does earn, he drinks. He's surviving primarily on Guinness and the potatoes he gets from neighbors. His work has never gone well here, whereas Owen's has thrived. In fact we've just gotten word that the play Owen finished in the spring will open at the Abbey Theatre this autumn; Harold's unable to share our excitement.

More and more he sticks to the West, that dire village and dark pub. Maybe he comes to Richard's pub less often because we're usually there and he needs an island audience to play off of. Maybe he dislikes the islanders we've grown closest to (Sean and Tommy have both spoken against him—awkward for us). Perhaps Harold even regrets having arranged for us to come, his own exclusivity as outsider now lost. And though Owen feels an affectionate loyalty to him, Harold's bitterness has made it hard for us to spend much time together. An unexpected sour note in our lives here.

An anticyclone has settled over the country—a stalled high-pressure system bringing glorious warm sunny weather. "The wind's gone round the clock," the men nod—a sign the weather's settled, though the route of the scant breeze is imperceptible to our unrefined senses. We've thrown all work aside to celebrate. But I actually heard a local respond to a tourist's praise of the fine weather by saying, "We'd want a bit of rain." The tourist asked, "How long *is* it since you've had rain here?" to which the islander complained, "Oh, two or three days . . ."

No such complaints from me. I've been swimming in the lovely, calm East Bay where there's no boating traffic and the water's clear enough to watch sea plants wavering on the white sand bottom. The East

Villagers watch me swim around and are amazed: no one on the island swims! Surrounded by water all their lives, always on it in boats, they're never taught to swim. Owen confesses he can't swim well either (half the reason for his reluctance in that rock pool?) and says that few in Ireland can. He says islanders (and all Ireland is an island) are fatalistic about the sea; if a boat goes down, best accept your fate and drown quickly rather than prolong the pain by trying, futilely, to save yourself. Many of the children have never seen a person swim and are jittery with excitement. They gather on the beach and stare and send messengers to summon their brothers and sisters. (A couple of years later, when another anticyclone came, ten of them asked for lessons and standing in a nervous circle around me learned to dunk their heads, float, and finally paddle about. It quickly became an island legend and is the thing I'm most remembered for by that generation now becoming adults.)

To cap this holiday spirit, the island's best musicians are home from England for their annual vacation. They are a strange crew, these returned islanders. They wear their city suits as a point of status and take pride in having trouble readapting to island ways. Only when they're drunk and take out their instruments or begin to sing are they truly islanders again.

What a loss they are to the island. An exquisite fiddler, an accordianist, and a singer. In former times they'd have been here to help the island sing itself through the year, not just two weeks of summer. The fiddler, Donal, a handsome, dark man in his early thirties, is especially talented. He plays in the true traditional fashion with verve and delicacy. When he lifts his fiddle to his chin, the room silences and he is transformed—an artist, a professional. And once in a while he sings in a mellow, plangent voice, a love ballad.

The more exciting singer is an older man, Martin, a ruffian sort, rotund, in his fifties. He has a robust, deep voice and a knack for lyrics. He's made up a long song about the island, sung to a traditional air, the chorus of which is:

> Oh you can go to Slyne
> And the Island of Lion
> From Clifden to old Letterfrack
>   Tick-tack!
> But don't go to the Cow
> Better turn back your bow
> Stephen Mannion don't know how to tack
>   Tick-tack!

Stephen Mannion is the island's fabled boatman—the old man we've yet to meet because he's been ill, the one who saved his boat and crew during The Disaster when every other boat was lost. Mockery of him in the chorus's last line is an inside joke that makes the islanders laugh uproariously every time the chorus comes round.

The verses to the song are a lengthy catalogue of abuse of the island, a heap of insults at its crudeness, oddness, and worthlessness. It's no place to go, everyone should leave, the song insists. No one knows how to do anything, the rain never stops, the houses leak, the chimneys smoke, there's nothing but spuds to eat. A terrible spot, the last place God made.

While the song is hilarious, it's also, of course, sad because within its satire lie bitter truths, and the man who's singing it left the island for England thirty years ago. It's especially odd for me who finds this place so beautiful. This pile of rocks has such magnetism for outsiders in spite of its own people's dismissal of its beauty or worth. And it's at its best now, with songs filling the pub all night, old men grabbing the hands of the singers and circling their arms in time with the rhythm, in the old fashion, as if helping to churn out the song. Feet stomp to the jigs, a céili (dance) is promised in the schoolhouse on Sunday night, and there are more smiles than I've seen in one room for ages.

But this unusual summer heat and gladness is a disruption in the lives of the islanders too. Theresa sails through the village still mummied in cardigans and greatcoat, sweating profusely. When I ask her why she doesn't put her woolens away for a while, she dodges my logic and says of the heat, "People isn't used to it. People is old." Sean is prone to depression—busy evenings are poignant reminders of lost happiness. He visibly dreads the departure of the visitors. His feelings pried open one night by drink, song, and the presence of old island friends, now successful abroad, he tearfully confessed that he'd once almost married. With more bitterness than I'd imagined him capable of, he told us the tale of his love for an island girl, his childhood sweetheart. But gossip split them—a busybody old woman who spread rumors of seeing them alone in the bog at night, and the girl's parents shipped her off to England. Five years later she married there, and Sean has never seen her since, nor loved another. His voice cracked. Owen muttered, "That's the way now." Sean whispered back, "That's for definite shur."

By the next night, though, Sean was joyful again, the music and reunion zest contagious. He's especially attached himself to our visiting friends, Nancy and Rick. Nancy's been my dearest friend since childhood, and it means so much to me that she and her husband have come to see us this first summer, to witness and share our lives here. So enthusiastic are they about the island that though they'd planned to stay only a week, they're staying for the rest of the summer, until the last moment possible before they must return to the States to begin law school. At last, here are friends who appreciate the island and who are willing to open themselves to its influence. I love watching their explorations and reactions and how Sean drolly answers their constant questions, never giving them the direct answers they relentlessly seek.

"Why are there so many rabbits here? Doesn't anyone ever eat them?"

Sean mutters, "Shur, the traps . . ."

"What kind of traps?"

"Shur, they're no good. Ye can't get a dacent trap around here. They're finished! The only place to get a dacent trap is in Dublin. But fair play to 'em, no one ever shot the rabbit."

"Why not?"

"Well, did ye ever hear tell of a man, Rick, who . . ."

And so the evenings stretch into the white nights and our voices rise as high as the larks do in the 4:00 A.M. sun, a joyful racket.

It still hasn't rained. Our rain barrel dried up and we now have to draw all our wash water from a stream about three-quarters of a mile east of us—Clossy, it's called, easier to reach than the well we go to for drinking water, a little stream by the crossroad along which the blackberries are about to explode into ripeness. If we're stringent, we can get by with a few trips a day. Most of it goes to the garden; we wear our clothes as long as possible and ration the rest for washing ourselves and the dishes.

We visit Catherine often, after dinner when things have quieted down a little. Nancy is especially touched by Catherine's strength and openness. She's the kind of woman, we think, we'd like to be when her age—her face lined with honest hard work, modesty, and grace. Appreciative of our company and occasional help in the kitchen, Catherine's been generous, giving us gallons of leftover milk from which to make our own cottage cheese. While we chat, Richard comes in on a break from the pub looking for an opportunity to tease the Americans. " 'Tis very late yur sleepin' these mornin's. I see them curtains still drawn when I go above milkin'. What, do ye's like stayin' in bed or somethin'?"

He belly-laughs, and Catherine, embarrassed at the innuendo, scolds theatrically: "Richard! How could you!"

Nancy glances at me with her eyes twinkling. She and Rick were noisily making love this morning and we wonder if Richard heard them. "It's all the hard work we're doing, Richard," I come back. "Tires us out."

"Sittin' and writin' is it? Ah shur, ye wouldn't know what hard work is. Never left the chair."

"Didn't you notice Owen cutting turf lately?"

"Cuttin' turf is it? I wouldn't call those fists of turf he knocked out of the ground *cut*. Shur, the man has never handled a spade in his life."

"Richard, stop talking nonsense." Catherine doesn't know how we'll take what's merely Richard's usual manner.

But I know Richard's humor well by now, and know how much is in fun, how much in deadly earnest. It's an advantage, in island terms, if someone mocks you outright, as Richard does. God only knows what's said about us out of earshot.

Nancy is amused by the repartee, my agility with it, and my slip into a pure Irish accent. Only talking to her again makes me aware of how much of an island voice and sensibility I've absorbed, how tremendously altered I am.

She laughs at how settled Owen and I are, says we couldn't be more "married," and that we don't look much like the rebels we were last spring. She watches with suspicion as I imply I have "problems" when obliquely probed by a neighbor as to why I don't have any children. And she wonders why I don't object when some of the men call me "Mrs." She's surprised to find me so tactful, discreet—it's not in my nature really. She also objects when we're intolerant of tourists in the bar, reminds us we're not long resident ourselves, and scolds us for not being more curious. But though she worries about the cost of some of our adjustments, she's susceptible to the island's power too. She and I have come out of the same world. That her reaction to the island is so like mine is a verification, a relief.

Haymaking and fishing. That's all anyone's doing these fine, hot end-of-summer days and evenings. The turf is stacked in big piles out on the bogs; it won't be carted home till the hay is cut and the fish barrels are full. In the sun-baked fields, the men wipe their brows, unfamiliarly sweaty, stale stout on their breath from breaks taken. Everyone is working, even the children. In this frantic scramble against the calendar's deadline (the scare of September), Owen and Rick, being two able-bodied men (not able-bodied idlers as Tommy unfavorably compares himself), have been drafted into full-time work. When working this way for a family, they are not paid, but fed—other women trundle out to them with sandwiches and tea. Nancy and I, meanwhile, fill our days tending to the garden, hauling water, and blackberrying.

The crossroad at Clossy is now an aisle of berries. There are bucketsful ripe and no one else is picking—they'd rather buy jam in the shop, twenty pence a jar. Nancy and I are determined that the berries shall

not go wasted. We share a passion for the life the islanders have discarded. Every one of its rituals pleases us,
makes us feel part of a large story we'd only read before.
The islanders are shocked and perhaps even a little
annoyed by our appetite for customs of which they're
ashamed. They find our zeal for free food embarrassing.
In dismissing what's around them for free because of
its commonness, though, they give up the freshest and
best food available—the island has a natural bounty that
to us is gourmet. Nightly we dine on shellfish, small
floury new potatoes, fresh vegetables, and blackberries.

Blackberry pies, blackberry cobblers, blackberry
muffins, blackberry pancakes, blackberry jam, or plain
blackberries and cream. Luckily no one's growing weary
of blackberries in our ménage, and the men devour
them in whatever form we've come up with on their
return from haymaking.

Most evenings they then go out fishing. This is
big-time, serious fishing for winter salting, and Nancy
and I are not welcome. The division of roles between
men and women has become rigid during this energetic
season. Given the amount that needs to get done, and
the rigor of the jobs the men must do, we don't feel
especially excluded though. Owen and Rick go out with
several old men from our village, experts who need a
couple of young men's clumsy strength to help them
out. They set nets at seven or so, then line-fish for a
couple of hours; then they pull the heavy nets in slowly,
untangling hundreds of caught fish, and not returning
to shore till the tail-end of twilight. They then clean,
wash, and throw preliminary salt on the fish they've
caught before tossing them into a barrel. The rest of
the salting process continues a few days later.

Owen and Rick come home after midnight, exhausted, hands cut and swollen, but like us exhilarated
by the work and the fruitfulness of it. Given Rick's

unabashed curiosity and enthusiasm, he always comes home laughing with tales to tell and with a big piece of driftwood balanced on his shoulder. One night, ten minutes behind Owen, he stopped to gaze at a white cow standing behind a high stone wall at the edge of the road. The cow was docilely staring west at the sunset, and Rick, in an act of homage to the island's totem, reached out to stroke her side. Startled, the cow bolted forward, and behind her Rick found her owner, our neighbor P.J., equally startled, sitting on a low stool, hands at udder level. Rick apologized for the interruption, but P.J. walked off muttering that he didn't understand why a man "would be goin' around touchin' heifers that was bein' milked."

This afternoon Rick inquisitively asked Tommy if they used Fahrenheit or Centigrade here. Tommy smiled wryly and said, "I don't know, to tell ye the truth, Rick. We just say it's a God-awful day."

Sunday morning is clear and calm. We're eating breakfast when Will comes to the door to say that a boat is leaving for Boar Island immediately after second mass. We'd promised the next fine Sunday for a return match in Boar, and this is it. Jack wants nothing to do with this trip, so a lobster boat is going from the East Bay. We're all delighted with the adventure.

We chug along for an hour and a quarter, the team, ref, fans, including Sean, and Joe Coyne as official documenter of the event. Boar Island's outlines slowly magnify in the sun. The white speck of a house on the southern slope becomes a house with windows and a gate. When we come into sight of the Boars, a flotilla of punts rushes out to meet us. Boar's quay is in such shallow water that large boats must always moor off-shore, so goods and passengers are ferried. When we land, we're greeted by half the population of the island.

Boar deserves its name—wild and bristly, the rock irredeemable, the roads in shambles. We climb up a cliff to the island's focal point—a schoolhouse and shebeen, the latter an illegal pub, no more than a shed storing cases of beer bought full-price on the mainland. Why Boar has not been allowed a pub by the government is a mystery. A big house beside the shebeen is home to an old man with two severe-looking daughters who are not at all pleased by our arrival. The husband of one of the women greets us enthusiastically though. It turns out he's from our island—Brendan's his name—and since marrying a Boar woman has moved back and forth between Boar and his home in a continuing wrangle with his wife, Agnes. He hates Boar and she hates the White Cow, so one of them compromises for a while, then the fights begin ("pitched battles," Sean calls them), and they change domicile.

The Boar football team gathers from several mountainy paths and leads us off to their pitch. We climb steep rocky hills and inch along precipitous cliffs, the sky and mood heady. Every time we pass a house, its inhabitants join our march, young and old trembly with excitement. The Boar houses are more desolate than ours, each one isolated, no cluster of a village, none freshly painted, most thatched. The yards are full of animals. They keep pigs and horses and sheep. They slaughter all their own meat—no imports here. And they grow all their own feed; every foot of arable land is sown with grain, turnips, or potatoes. Boar is largely self-sufficient, as our own island was not so long ago. There is hardly a sign of the twentieth century on it. Even the White Cow's relative progressiveness, seven miles away, has not touched this island, it's so effectively cut off from outsiders and influences. A priest tries to come to say mass every other week from the mainland but often fails because of the weather. The mail comes up once a week through Jack, but in winter it's usually a month between trips. It's hard to imagine Catherine growing up here, going on to England, and doing all she's done since. Perhaps desperation for escape is the source of all her drive. We meet her father, a fit man in his eighties, who joins our climb to watch the match. I have a small package for him, some clothes Catherine asked me to bring up; he accepts them with embarrassment and uses them as a cushion at the field.

The Boars are impressive folk in the best West of Ireland tradition. The infertility of their island only makes them more determined to grow crops on it. The White Cow's greater richness has induced indulgence. There's strength and character and openness in these faces—I recognize Catherine's tenacity, curiosity, and energy. But the Boars seem slightly sad, aware now of how much they're missing out on, the extremity of their isolation. They cling to us, starved for social life.

The football field is in a deep, windy natural amphitheater in the middle of the island, bound to lend Olympian proportions to the contest. A narrow stream cuts across part of it—a minor inconvenience, a skeptical Owen is assured. Nancy, Rick, and I and the others take our seats on the slope. Less rivalry in the air this time, though Boar is itching for victory. Pride and hospitality are more the order of the day, especially because of us outsiders and because of men like Sean and Joe Coyne who haven't been to Boar in years. "A great day, a great day," the men keep declaring with genuine joy.

Below, in a dream, the boys play football, dodging stones and the stream. Owen runs about gleefully and the audience cheers. "Our men will show ye how the game is played this time," a Boar shouts down. Birds hover above the clamor while clouds stroll benignly by. Fittingly, the Boars win and even our team doesn't mind, having won before, and because now we can head back to the shebeen. We stand around outside the shed with bottles of beer, recollecting the already legendary first match. The evening chills after a few drinks, but the Boars don't want to let us leave, and besides, we're all starving by this time. So Agnes is embarrassed into offering a snack—walloping black tea and delicious bread baked in the pot oven by the turf fire, thick-crusted with a slight smoky tinge to it. This act of generosity is excruciating to Agnes. She stares glumly into the fire while the whole White Cow contingent takes turns at her table.

A great visit, a great trip, all agree amidst much handshaking on the quay. "Yur welcome back any time now," to us. And we just may make another trip. Owen has managed to talk to a man we'd heard has a curragh for sale, old but in good condition. We've been talking about getting a boat of our own and everyone advised, "It's a curragh ye want," the traditional boat of the coast—a marvelously buoyant, keelless craft made of tarred canvas stretched over a canoe-like frame. It's rowed with long narrow oars which are almost bladeless. The boat's so well balanced and rides so lightly on the water that the slightest touch of the oars controls her, even in rough seas. In inept hands, though, she's inclined to turn round in circles. Still, despite our unfamiliarity with the art of curragh rowing, she was deemed the safest boat for us, and Jack, resident expert, pointed us north to a triple-named O'Toole for a secondhand bargain.

The man in question answered our inquiry with a pipe stuck in his teeth and his eyes cast somewhere over in County Mayo. He said it wasn't his boat actually, but he might pass on word of our interest to the owner. "But there's definitely a boat for sale?" Owen queried. No, he wouldn't say that exactly, but there was a boat and he supposed it might be sold for the right price. "And what would that be?" He'd no idea. Owen said he'd be in touch, and the man said there'd be no harm in that. Some kind of negotiations are in progress, Owen's confident.

Loud song-making all the way home in the swooping twilight. Will had stuck his melodeon in the wheelhouse before leaving and now needs no encouragement to play. Joe Coyne proudly documents that there wasn't a match played on Boar in twelve years, and isn't today's trip a great thing. Sean has an arm over each of our shoulders and we sway as we sing. The lights of the island begin to come on, and a donkey greets us from a far northeastern promontory of bog while a committee gathers on the short pier of the East Village to receive the boat's rope, the score, news of the journey.

Nancy and I go down to Bridget's to shop and she insists we come into the kitchen for coffee. Coffee instead of tea because we're Americans. Lately she's begun stocking small jars of instant coffee in the shop. The price is exorbitant, but the islanders have been snatching them up to serve to their visiting relations—Yanks routinely showing up in plaid pants and Aran sweaters bought duty-free at Shannon. The women offer to make them handmade ones, taking out tapes to measure their chests, and the visitors promise to send things from the States, cassette recorders and digital clocks that run off batteries. A cousin of Maura's has just turned up with a car for her. "Now she'll banish the old one and leave it sittin' out to rot on the beach, a misery to all who look on it," Bridget wails. "Well, she'd need no car if she stayed home at night with her children as by rights she should." The usual denigration of our one female alcoholic.

Bridget sits us down at the kitchen table. I try to dissuade her from cutting three kinds of bread and cake and filling bowls with butter and jam, but she's not to be swayed. "Ye'll sit," she insists—meaning an elaborate afternoon tea rather than the more usual "cup in the hand" of tea alone. Bridget bustles around proudly, wiping out a jug to fill with fresh creamy milk, pleased to have the chance to welcome my guest. Her hospitality today is meant to show Nancy how close she and I are, to imply we have coffee together every time I shop. And it's meant to show me how much she cares for me—that she's willing to go to such trouble to make my friend think that. It's also just to show Nancy what fine people I live among—the islanders go to great lengths to outdo one another in the matter of hospitality. During this season of constant visitors, they always have a cake or two waiting in the dresser just in case someone drops by, though when someone does, they apologize for having nothing in the house, only this old bit of a cake, but what would you expect in "this mountainy place."

"I hope ye's don't mind the instant coffee now, I know yur used to better in America." We assure her we love it though we'd have been much happier, of course, with Irish tea. "I love the coffee breaks in America now. Anytime ever I'm visiting my daughters in Long Island—now that's a different class of an island than this one, I'll tell ye!—as soon as ever they've put in an hour's work at something, they're away sayin', 'Let's have a cup of coffee, Mammy.' And the fine cup it is

140

too. They'd always have it sittin' there warm in the pot and ready for when they're talkin' on the phone or watchin' the telly. I wouldn't mind a cup of it right now one bit." Bridget's happy for this opportunity to indulge in her American rhapsody, and happy too when she has to get up midsentence to see to her calling husband, just to prove how hard her life is. "He won't let me be a single minute, that man. Why we women are always goin' off marryin' I haven't a clue. Wouldn't we be happy as the fish leapin' in the sea on our own."

A huge fire blazes in Bridget's hearth. Even in this balmy summer weather, the insides of the houses are damp and chilly, years of cold stubborn in the stones. No matter how high the fire's piled, Bridget says, it doesn't keep her warm. Her son complains that he'll be "kilt drawin' turf for 'er." On a nail from the mantel hangs a string of rosary beads. When she's left alone, Bridget sits close in to the fire talking to them with her knobby fingers.

"Ye'd want to have four hands, really and truly ye would now," Bridget returns. "And it wouldn't hurt a bit to have the few amenities either." "Amenities" is a word that's only recently shown up in the island vocabulary, encompassing all the conveniences we lack. "Ye'd really want the refrigerator now in this heat. Shur the milk's gone off completely from one milkin' to the next."

A woman with a withered leg limps by on the road. As she passes the kitchen window, Bridget hushes and we wait silently. Once she's out of range, Bridget throws back her head in mild disgust and sighs, "Ah shur."

"Who's that?" Nancy asks.

I prepare myself for an embarrassing tirade.

"Shur that girl's carryin' the curse of God on her. She was born with the leg gone bad and why

141

wouldn't she be considerin' the mother that was in it."

"Who's her mother?"

"Ach, old Mary Collins who was never married a'tall and wouldn't say who the father was though the whole world knew it was Paddy Boyle. The two of 'em makin' out like it was an immaculate conception—hah! She was walkin' around with her nose high in the air for nine months. Well she lowered it a peg when the child was born and it with the sick leg. She knew then she'd been punished and the child would carry the mark of it forever. She changed her tune then. The poor girleen, she never had a chance."

"What does she do now?"

"There's just the two of 'em in it now, she takes care of the old mother. No one on the island would be fool enough to marry her."

Nancy looks at me, saddened. I've heard the story in a number of versions already and by now I've become inured to these stories of painful, wasted lives. Nancy waits for my reaction, my protest, but it doesn't come.

"There are things on this island ye haven't heard the half of," Bridget warns. "We'd be a week talkin' if I was to tell ye's them all. But believe ye me, they make out they're very holy, but they're as low as the rat in the tide if ye ask me. Shur there was hardly a woman married in the last ten years didn't have the first child six months after. And those are the first ones ye see paradin' into mass every mornin' of the week. It's enough to make ye sick!"

Mr. Joe Coyne, keeper of histories and weaver of fabulous lies, is dead. Sean found him yesterday morning on the floor of his kitchen after noticing no smoke from his chimney the day and night before. He and Richard broke down the door, Catherine and the priest in attendance close behind.

The historian died in filth and torment after a fall (following a stroke, Catherine guesses) surrounded by 280 pounds in small bills he'd just gotten for cattle sold on the mainland and covered with tar from a two-gallon can knocked over as he fell.

The island's abuzz with the news, especially the laying bare of the secret life of the house this sudden death affords. Sean came by bristling with details: not a scrap of food in the place, no clothes but the ones he was wearing, no sheets, no blankets—he slept between two moldy feather mattresses. But 2,000 pounds in cash was found locked in a table drawer with a yellowed note leaving it all to a nephew in England.

We marveled at how well he'd looked just last weekend on the trip to Boar. But Sean said he'd seen Joe Coyne two days after (Sean already legending) and Joe had muttered something about taking sleeping pills sent in from town. Sean told him he'd be better off "with his own sleep" no matter "how little was in it."

While Sean helped Catherine clean the corpse for burial, two cousins arrived and "ramsacked" the house. Piles of rubbish had been hoarded for years. Sean catalogued: "Every kind of junk ye could imagine that was ever washed ashore, tins and plastic and ropes, and a broken electric kettle of Catherine's that he must've lifted from her trash, 10,000 jam jars and Lucozade bottles, and 700,000 letters from all over the world. If a lad was born tomorrow, he'd be gettin' the pension and still tryin' to finish readin' those letters."

Today is the funeral, our first on the island. The islanders are great funeral-goers. A crowd gathers expectantly outside the church half an hour before the mass begins. Inside, the Oriental trappings of the mass set an exotic mood—incense, high, tinkling gold bells, the silken robes of the priest—so at odds with the rock and inrushing tide just beyond the chapel door.

"He lived a full life," the women console themselves. "God rest 'im," the men mutter while twitching their heads, uninclined to talk of death. The sun's too gloriously bright for a funeral. The men's minds are on hay. Donkeys bray in the fields as we assemble outside and form a procession. Men to the fore, a knot around the plain wood coffin—the few relations closest, and next, community leaders who must be honored with a turn in the pallbearing, Richard among them, Sean too, as neighbor. They take turns, six at a time, carrying the coffin to the cemetery a mile and a half to the east ("The coffin was as light as a girl's," Sean reports after. "A pity."). Women take up the rear in small groups, whispering—official reverence and subdued, girlish joy of occasion competing on their kerchief-framed faces. Owen and I and Nancy and Rick walk at the boundary between the men and the women so that we may walk together.

The priest's robes billow lightly and the sun glints off his clerical jewels. Donkeys push to the edges of fields to gawk. The coffin bobs ahead in high view. Everyone ambulatory on the island is now part of the motley line, this final walk with the dead; even those who weren't at the mass join in, leaping over ditches from their fields as the procession passes. It must be moving for islanders to know that for them too such a walk will be made, an accompaniment to the grave by every walking person on the island.

But real feelings fall short of the scope of the ritual, at least in a case like this for an eccentric old man not much in touch with his neighbors and without close relations. I suppose we valued his tales much more

than the islanders, who'd heard them all a hundred
times before. And the day is really too joyous for a
funeral, too astir with hay and birds and wild flowers.

Every time the pallbearers change shift, the procession stumbles into itself and waits. Finally, at the
cemetery, we head for the opened grave. But surprisingly, most of the islanders scatter in various directions
and stand in small groups far from the final resting
place of Joe Coyne. We learn that this is an island custom—every family stands by the graves of its own dead,
most out of earshot of the priest's litany, praying for
their own.

Joe Coyne's grave is filled in during the recitation of the rosary and covered with the stones that were
displaced in the digging. A scatter of winkle shells is
left above-ground—"That's what the monks ate, the
graveyard's full of 'em," Tommy whispers to me, already
stepping into the old historian's shoes. We file out,
women heading home, men to the pub. And as the last
stones were being placed on Joe Coyne's grave, Sean
swears, a cousin of the just-buried man slipped out, and
by the time we hit the road was driving cattle into his
newly available fields.

Negotiations were made on the sodden, circuitous (island to mainland to island) telephone line to Boar, and
finally a price was set and we were summoned to pro-
cure our curragh. We hired Jack for a Sunday afternoon run and towed the curragh home, a nineteen-foot
feather bobbing at the tail of the big boat. A major
event for the island—a new boat—and a bevy of men
met us on the quay to inspect her. "She'll want a coat

of tar, that's for shur." "That gunwale there's a disgrace." "Ah what did the Boars ever know about buildin' curraghs anyways?" But all in all she was adjudged a sound craft, a good light curragh, just the thing for our needs, and good value. "The Boars are fair men, I'll say that for 'em," Jack nodded, presiding.

We made a mooring for her in the harbor, a spot where we can keep watch on her from the top of the hill. Compulsively, we walk out to the crest to glance at her every time the wind shifts. At high tide she spins and points; at low, she leans on her side with the others, temporarily land bound. Already Owen and Rick have begun to fish in her and this morning brought in fifty mackerel for Nancy and me to clean and salt. Now they're out again with a twelve-year-old island boy, Ciaran, who's offered his expertise about fishing grounds in exchange for the free ride. Nancy and I, meanwhile, have taken over the hotel.

Catherine collapsed the other night—exhaustion, nerves, and an arthritic hip acting up—and was taken off the island on a stretcher, leaving responsibility in our inexperienced hands. An unprecedented breakdown of the island's great powerhouse. "My heart's broken cooking for this crowd," were her last words to us, "completely broken." Three meals a day for sixty-five! We're overwhelmed and uneasy with our charge—outsiders suddenly installed as bosses—but the staff, luckily, seems to work by rote, so we simply stay out of their way. Catherine always does the desserts and breads, though, so they're left to us. First we translate our American recipes into British measures, then, multiplying everything by 10 or 12, we find ourselves doing things like breaking three dozen eggs into a bowl; no doubt we need a course in hotel management. The staggering amount of food makes it a game to us, but an exhausting one—I don't know how Catherine ever manages it.

146

When the dishes are washed and dried and finally put away for the night (the island girls don't understand the dishwasher Catherine bought and still do them by hand), Nancy and I climb up to the "Black Gate," a meeting spot just above the hotel on the way to our village, a gate that was always black in the past but which Richard, when he acquired the field beyond it, perversely painted white; nevertheless, the black monicker sticks. From the Black Gate we can observe the whole harbor and a long stretch of the low road. It's eleven, still bright, and a loose air of festivity's abroad. Men and children out walking, riding bikes, standing talking. Below, Owen and Rick are just in from fishing, cleaning out a net Sean lent them that is bulging with fish—cod, ling, pollock, glacog, rockfish, crab, mackerel, one Franach, and three huge, writhing eels. Young Ciaran has jumped from our curragh to a punt of Richard's and is rowing around the harbor, loath to leave the water even after four hours. We laugh, watching Owen and Rick fight off gulls swooping at the net. In Richard's field a rooster mounts a hen, corncrakes commence their cranky twilight crepitations, and the milk hitting the pail in the barn sings to us.

At the hotel, vacationing, is a woman who's drama critic for one of the Dublin papers. She was anxious to meet Owen, so we made a party of it—Tommy, Sean, some tourists from Belfast, and a few island neighbors.

Sean arrived at the door with a bag of onions as party offering, the way one might bring a bottle of wine, and settled into a dark corner. Catrina, the critic, is young, blond, vivacious, and witty, so Tommy took to her at once. Thrilled to be in the mainstream again for the first time since his banning, he cemented himself to Catrina's side and passed around a flask of poteen he'd brought, rapidly getting us all jarred. At least for once Tommy was pursuing a woman who could take care of herself in such situations—Tommy's a "type" Catrina no doubt knows well, whereas Nancy was thrown embarrassingly off guard by his public advances just as I first was. "Keep that arm close to the body God made it for and off of me," Catrina roared at him in a sharp Dublin accent that made us giggle. We all took to her at once for her humor and warmth. But when she and Owen talked alone, they spoke a secret language of quick Dublin wit that left me in the dark.

Tommy told the story of The Disaster for Catrina's sake, his arm around her shoulder, his face close to her rouged cheek, while Sean monitored the facts with an eagle eye from the corner, irritated by Tommy's performance. Then Catrina turned away toward Owen to talk Abbey Theatre politics while the rest of us got progressively drunker. Owen suddenly broke into song, a traditional Gaelic tune he's been crooning around the house, and Sean, rising, followed with a ballad: "It was only a bunch of violets, a bunch of violets blue"—a lament for lost love. Then Catrina sang very sweetly what she said was her current "party song" (lengthy preparations go into these spontaneous outbursts), "She Moves Through the Fair." We each sang in turn, "The Camptown Races" requested of the Americans, "doo-dah, doo-dah," then dragged out the little record player Nancy and Rick had brought us as a gift—a battery-operated blue plastic one designed for children—and put on a Chieftains record. Sean, tremendously impressed with the apparatus, jumped up to dance, and I kicked back the chairs to dance with him. We spun, stomped, and hooted, the music infectious. Sean was handsome and young again, letting his heels fly, gleeful. His eyes were as bright as the East Village Bay under the morning sun and his big hardened hands held my shoulders tenderly. I could almost have fallen in love with him.

Catrina reluctantly agreed to take a spin with Tommy, but sometime during the dance, Tommy went too far and Catrina gave him a shove and shouted, "Go away out of that! I've had my bellyful of you!" Tommy stumbled over a chair and landed on the floor, stunned. The party froze. Owen went over to help him up, but Tommy glared, furious at the public insult, and stamped out. Too drunk to stand up straight, he fell in the road just beyond the gate, then quickly got up and disappeared.

Catrina was apologetic, but we assured her she hadn't offended us—he'd only gotten what he had coming. Still, it put a damper on the evening and everyone drifted out shortly after.

Today Tommy stood on the quay sullen, detached. He claimed to have hurt his arm when he fell and moped at our lack of concern. "I wouldn't say much for your friends, Deba. Well, I wouldn't say much for meself either, matter of fact. Shur, the whole thing's washed up." The tourist season is over and Tommy has nothing to look forward to—no free drinks from charmed visitors, no woman magically appearing to rescue him from his unbearable loneliness. It's the end of summer, the end of the year's possibility.

Autumn

Summer is gone away with all its joys and sorrows, some people glad of it, other people sad of it, but that's the way of the world. Autumn has arrived. I hope it will bring peace and happiness to us, soon again winter. Is not it strange?

—Eibhlís Ní Shúilleabháin,
Letters from the Great Blasket

'Tis a winter's day and has the cut of it. . . .
The rocks that jut out of the sea are all out of
sight because of the storm and swirling foam
which has swallowed them up. The grass,
which yesterday was green, is all faded today.
The very skin on your face is changing because of the bad weather. The sheep on the
hill are driven from their shelter and are trying to make their way right in onto the hearth.
The fish that disported itself and basked in
the sun almost on the surface has disappeared. . . .

—Tomás O'Crohan

 An equinoctial gale: out of the clear calm of
the anticyclone, with none of the usual por-
tents, a fierce force nine gale, rainless. It is
the angle of the earth, says Sean, the autumn
equinox, nothing to do with weather, but transition.
The worst gale we've yet experienced, deafening, dry,
and eery. The windows clatter, the green beans are
stripped from their vines in half an hour, and hens
won't come out of their barrels. A no-egg day.

Twenty-four hours later, it stops as abruptly as it
began. In one moment, the sun comes out, the ritual is
over. Summer again. But for how long? Tenuous end-
of-summer, the new season official, its premiere a re-
hearsal for more. Sean says the drought will soon break.
Nancy and Rick are leaving tomorrow, just in time.
Their stay has coincided with the six weeks of summer. They wonder how we'll survive such gales. They
doubt that the island out of its holiday phase is a place
they could endure. They worry for us.

"Thank God we're surrounded by water," the
men sing arrogantly in the pub, still caught up in sum-

mer's festival and bolstering their gumption to face the departure of the tourists and the coming winter. It's the refrain to a song popular all over Ireland, but more piquant here. "We're an island off an island off an island," Tommy hisses, denigrating us on the basis of detachment from the European mainland, conveniently denigrating England as well. But "Thank God we're surrounded by water!" he shouts when the chorus comes round, as if water could protect us, hold the world at bay.

This water that surrounds us is still fit for a curragh in inexperienced hands. So today, with the sea pond-calm, we finally made a pilgrimage to the Gentle Island to the south, our evacuated neighbor. It has no harbor to speak of, no quay. We land in a slit between boulders, climb bare-faced rock, rope in hand, and tie the boat to a rusty pipe jammed into a crevice. The island's animal life explodes in panic—a small flock of sheep put here by a Cow Islander runs for its life and birds protest in loud confusion as we walk toward the village.

Or what was the village, and still appears to be from a distance, the houses intact, clustered, backs turned against the threat of the southwest. No smoke rising from these chimneys, though.

As we reach the first house, we fall back, shy of invasion. The curtains are pulled open, the door unlocked, and inside, the table is still littered with breakfast dishes from the last morning of habitation of the Gentle Island sixteen years ago. Tongs are propped by the hearth, armchairs turned in for warmth before it. Steamless, the kettle is poised on the stove. The cupboard's lined with tins and boxes, and a melodeon, extended and full of stale air, is drooped over a table. Nothing taken, nothing altered. Nothing brought out for the new life on the mainland. For sixteen years the house has sat like this, frozen in its final day. House after house it's the same.

None of us knows the people of these houses, but we are mute with a sense of their loss. Distressed, we wander the ghostly museum of the island, a memento mori inadvertently created by the reluctance of the people to move on.

This isn't Ireland's only abandoned island—a number of islands have died this century, most notably the Great Blasket. Blasket's death throes succeeded in capturing the imagination of the Irish populace because the island was blessed with several extraordinary writers—Peig Sayers, Tomás O'Crohan, Maurice O'Sullivan, and Eibhlís Ní Shúilleabháin—who documented what life had been there and what it had become. Blasket had always lived precariously; there was no priest, no nurse or doctor, and the people eked out a subsistence from fishing. "Six of my children survived," is all Peig Sayers says to summarize the first decade of her arranged marriage. All the Blasket books are chronicles of losses.

In scores of letters to a friend in Dublin who had spent time on the island years before, Eibhlís Ní Shúilleabháin poignantly documented the final days of Blasket.

> Another house has been closed on the Island lately. She was an old woman—the Kearneys' mother—and she went out to her daughters. . . . So picture our Island home sinking from day to day.
>
> —August 1940

> A notice came to the teacher to close the school at once from the Parish Priest so next day she bid the Islanders adieu after about seven easy years teaching and left the three poor scholars to run wild with the rabbits, which is their de-

light indeed. I hear they will be sent out to some outside school and that the Government will pay for their board.

—June 1941

We have determined at last to leave this lovely Island, I know you will be very sad to hear it, but things are not as they should be and times are changed and especially for us here with a child at school age and no school and people saying and telling us the child must go to school very soon. They may take her away somewhere when they think of it you would know, so we thought it best to go out somewhere ourselves and try and have at least one joy out of this hard life, to live with our child. So the next time you will come to this Island there will not be no Eibhlís but the ruins of the house, only the walls as we are taking out the head [roof]. . . . Whatever happens on this Island I have one gifted thing to tell you of it I was always happy there. I was happy among sorrows on this Island. I think I will not be interesting in life atall from this on when I am gone out on the Mainland.

—February 1942

Brendan Kiely says: "The Great Blasket is empty because community life seemed no longer possible there, the people no longer prepared to face up to a primitive way of living, lacking amenities" (that word rearing its bland head again) "and comforts that people elsewhere had become accustomed to; and because Europe was dying at the fringes."

This is the old edge of the Old World and it crumbles under our feet. On this ghost island, where leaks and draughts go unattended, and screeching cormorants answer their own echoes with more screeches, no human sound is at home. The Great Blasket was at least memorialized by its last people. Here there is nothing left and nothing to remember by.

Could the Island of the White Cow ever be reduced to this? The thought is devastating. But certainly it's the direction it's moving, with the population declining yearly as the old people die and few newborns replace them. There's no economy to speak of, no reason really that the island has to continue to exist. The White Cow has always assumed its good harbor will ensure its survival, make it an important island, as in the past. But how important is an island harbor now that the fishing industry's so diminished? "No more daring, intrepid seamen exist," a priest here had saluted the Gentle Islanders who overcame their bad harbor for centuries. The government could easily justify evacuating the White Cow too in order to eliminate a school and a medical service and a parish. How many archaic little places will the government continue to find it expedient to support?

Peig Sayers knew the old life of the islands wouldn't last past her own time: "People will yet walk above our heads; it could even happen that they'd walk into the graveyard where I'll be lying but people like us will never again be there. We'll be stretched out quietly—and the old world will have vanished."

The beauty of the day and the lush hills and bright cliffs of the Gentle Island only make us gloomy; we row back in silence. No fish bite as I halfheartedly drag a line behind us. The sea is empty, unstirred, an accumulating quiet that is too much like the quiet of the Gentle Island.

Tomorrow the last couple dozen tourists are departing en masse. Abruptly, an exodus that will leave the island stilled. Already the grief of abandonment hangs over the island's face, and ours too as we must say good-bye to Nancy and Rick, who have shared our lives here so completely. We are relieved, though, to be staying, not to be among those who keep coming and leaving, but to be the ones left behind.

The mail boat will sail less frequently—boat traffic is the season's measure. "Is she in yet?" Jim-John will anxiously ask as he comes from his fields trying to gain view of the harbor from our crest. Has successful contact with the world been made? Has anything arrived? Is the day's communication with the world now over?

She draws her silent diagonal to the mainland, a smudge of blue on the big grey that separates us, a little trail of silver faintly visible behind her. She grows smaller, then slips out of sight into Clochan Bay; we are left alone.

Already the land has lost its summer bounty, withered by drought and hay-cutting. New birds have appeared to work the stubbled fields: sea-pies, black with white breasts and bright orange beaks. They line up like infantry, all facing southeast, and march forward eating everything edible in their path. They ravage a field in a matter of hours, corner to corner. They are like a mopping-up operation, a chilling sign of the end of summer. Where have they come from and how did they know these fields were ready?

Fair day in Clifden, the first big fair of autumn when the jobbers come from all over Connaught to see the best of Connemara's cattle. Terrific traffic on the road all morning, cattle haltered and docilely following their excitable owners down to the quay. A crowd of men and cattle clomping on the concrete, children loitering be-

hind some old boats to watch, their school satchels ig-
nored on their backs. Jack brings the boat to float at
the quay, worried—the tide's begun to ebb and more
than a dozen bullocks and three horses have to be
loaded before he gets grounded there. Jamesy explodes
into action as soon as the boat's tied, throwing off all
the hatches to the hold and constructing a pulley with
ropes tied to the mast. Someone's brought a cartload
of hay and he's handing it down to Jack in the hold to
spread over the floor. "Aright, Mick, bring your bashte
(beast), come on now, there's no time for delayin'." An
excited Mick drags his bullock forward. The animal
gets nervous near the edge of the quay and pulls back,
whining. He's steadied, parallel to the boat, and
Jamesy and the owner throw a blanket around his
middle, then the doubled rope of the pulley is looped
over him. Two young men jump down to the boat
behind Jamesy. They draw the slack of the pulley till
it tightens around the animal's body. Hangers-on burst
forward to steady the bullock who panics at the first tug.
Now Jamesy and the two young men pull down on the
rope with their whole bodies, knees nearly touching the
deck, and the bullock's middle lifts. He bellows with
pain and terror and flails his feet. The owner and help-
ers hold him in place. With the next hoist his feet lift
off the ground and he shrieks pitifully. Anxiety and
thrilled mutters on the quay, the other beasts fidgety or
downright rebellious in the face of this spectacle. One
tries to escape and is contained by the group of truant
children. When the bullock's fully aloft, though, he
goes passive, as if his fate is sealed. His half-ton's weight
swings toward the deck as the three men on the pulley
hoist him higher. He's mute, motionless, midair above
the hatch, when swiftly and smoothly the pulley's re-
versed with shouts of instruction ("Slow down, ye's";
"Steady now") from the quay and the hold where Jack

and a couple of others wait to receive the cargo—"Watch his back leg!" "*Shtop!*" The bullock disappears below deck. Clatter and fuss as his feet hit the floor and his weight's his own again, his life temporarily reprieved. The blanket and rope are torn off and thrown up for the next victim. One after another they're brought forward mooing, lifted and lowered, shrieking then silent, the crowd hypnotized and none of the men doing the prodigious work any worse for wear, the eventfulness lending them strength. Their authority and prowess is impressive—it's a task done only a few times a year, yet they take to it as if it were daily work.

The horses are saved for last and are much more resistant than the cattle. The first one leaps into the air when he feels the rope, pulls violently, kicks. A half-dozen men are needed to control him. He neighs and screeches so abysmally that I can hardly bear to stay. But I'm the only one with this reaction. The islanders are excited by the ritual and indifferent to the routine suffering of animals. Their attitude is so at odds with my Americanized notions. Almost all the island sheep, horses, and donkeys are tethered, front leg tied to back, to shorten their strides and keep them from swift escapes. No one thinks twice about hurling a stone at a dog or a horse to control it. Most kittens and puppies are drowned at birth—after-the-fact birth control on this animal-crowded island.

There's a genuine mood of celebration as the boat pulls out on its way to the Clifden Fair, hatches wide open, the backs of beasts visible in the cramped quarters below, their owners standing around on deck, smoking. On shore, we are braced by the cold breeze and this unusual morning gathering. We drift into the pub though it's only ten in the morning. No one will work today.

But later I'm moved to write. Before I came to the island I wrote poems as a traveler passing through the landscape in a blur, imagining lives behind windows abstractly as if they were foreign artifacts. Given the protective middle-class world I moved in, any life unlike my own *was* foreign. I began to hate being outside, part of the passing traffic. I knew as a writer I had to get inside, hear and see firsthand; now at last I do. Today's poem:

Crossing

"Islands are great places," he'd say,
"Till you want to get off."
And he should know, driving
a wedge of a boat
in and out of that channel, decades.

But who knew better
than the horses
lowered into the hold
on a pulley strung from the mast,
the horses who always gave up
their thrashing when,
hooves finally lifted free of the pier,
they swung full-bodied
in salt air, swallowing sure catastrophe.
They never walked the same on mainland.

Miracle of miracles. Tommy is in love and someone is in love with Tommy. A tail-end tourist, spunky English woman, who was a nun in a silent order for eleven years until last winter. Maria's her name. Every night this week they've been seen drinking cheek-to-cheek in the West Village pub, the talk of the island, she ablush and Tommy a new man—jovial, helpful, his gossip benign. The summer's yearning has produced.

I wonder what she sees in him, as unlike as they are. Unless he is all her longings for freedom, noise, and wildness, the embodiment of her rebellion, just as Owen was for me . . .

Mrs. Gaskell quoted on the BBC on the problem of woman as artist: "What you must do, my dear, is this: always soak the laundry overnight and put dinner in the oven in the morning." Is this any kind of modern solution? I loiter in bed with tea, smoking Gauloise cigarettes a tourist left behind, daydreaming. In some ways I'm relieved the summer is over, all our guests gone, though I miss Nancy and Rick. The price of guests is an endless round of cooking and dishes and laundry, all such an ordeal here. Food becomes an obsession—obtaining it, storing it, transforming it. Even now, planning for winter, we spend hours of conversation on food, worrying if our store of vegetables and salted fish will see us through. Catherine has promised to help out however she can. She is back, recovered, and her gratitude for our rescue job in the hotel has cemented our friendship. She knows how marginal our existence is—more out of necessity than choice most of the time. The ethic behind our decisions is utterly mysterious to her, but she is completely accepting.

Catherine is the only woman on the island I can come close to talking honestly to. We tread around the taboos our different backgrounds and generations throw between us. With me, Catherine can laugh now at her old hysteria about separating unmarried couples in the hotel and being kept up nights by opening and closing doors. We bring ourselves closer—she draws me toward the island, I draw her toward the outer world she's so curious about and excited by. We meet on fortuitous middle ground.

We've been off the island for ten days, in Dublin, for the opening of Owen's play at the Abbey. Leaving was painful. We made what we guessed would be a last call on Mrs. O'Malley; for, investigating what Mrs. O'Malley termed an "arm complaint," Catherine discovered a massive tumor in her breast and armpit, an advanced cancer that Catherine said would kill her within a couple of weeks. As soon as she admitted her illness, Mrs. O'Malley disintegrated, and she is now, quite suddenly, a dying woman. A nephew has taken over in the post office and Mrs. O'Malley receives visitors a few hours a day in "the room," a parlor unused since her husband's death.

An unlit, lugubrious room, probably cherished for its mahoganies and plump damask cushions, now cushions of dust. We went with a fruitcake, were formally served port in tiny crystal glasses, and talked of radishes and bad chimneys as if nothing were amiss.

We sailed out the next morning, sadly watching the island recede. Departing from the island is slow torture—stepping off it onto the boat, then watching for a full hour as home grows gradually, increasingly distant. What is it in us that wants to dwell on islands, to be cut off from the world, to feel, inversely, cut off when on the mainland, cut off from the island which is our only center? Stepping out onto the mainland, entering that other realm, the water between mainland and island seemed like a threshold beyond our navigation. At that moment, it was hard to believe the island reattainable. All difficulties faded as we gazed back, severed.

Humming in the wires. Unfamiliar sounds we immediately noticed on the mainland, the normal business of the world. The land looked vast after living so long on a minute clump of it. Mountains, roads, patches of spruce and pine from reforestation efforts, so much substantiality broken only by the blue eyes of lakes. Fifty miles of winding boggy road to Galway, the mountains shifting arrangement with every turn, their colors thrown down from the sky—one of the most magnificent stretches of road in Ireland. Clouds changed shape and hue over our shoulders as we moved away from the sea.

A train to catch in Galway, a schedule to keep to—it was nerve-wracking. Synge says that in the Aran Islands, in the early part of the century, there was no conception of time at all by hours. Shadows were the only measure. On a cloudy day, mealtimes were guesswork. And those islanders came to this same city of Galway to sell cattle and buy horses as islanders do today to buy shoes and oil heaters. Galway is full of those come in from the hinterlands, their carved country faces standing out in relief from the smoothed-over townspeople's. Dreamily adrift in a world of hours, wandering across streets forgetting to look first, they raise shouts and sneers.

We were as much in shock as any of them after we pulled in, courtesy of a young Galway salesman returning from his rounds in the West. Market town bustle: the noise level bone-rattling, a cacophony of accents and languages, exchange of money the only clear-cut form of communication. We rushed across town to the station, dodging traffic inexpertly, and collapsed onto the last train out to Dublin.

The Dublin stay was dismal. To be in a city again, particularly one with so little to redeem its grating noise and dirt, was an impossible adjustment. The rain-grey streets and identical modern pubs and crying tinker children overwhelmed any residual charm the city has. I found it tattered and glum. I'd only been in Dublin once before, when we'd first arrived in Ireland. We'd gotten a cheap charter flight to London, then hitchhiked through Wales to the Dublin ferry. After a sleepless night on it, we pulled in by train to Westland Row at dawn. Owen was electric with the excitement of return and kept pointing out faces and snatches of conversation on the boat and train as being "quintessentially Irish," as if giving me a crash course during the last few hours before I'd step out onto Irish soil myself.

I followed one "quintessentially Irish" young woman with my eyes—her long, angular face and jutting chin, black hair, and deeply somber expression. She left the station, walked past a church, crossed herself, then went into an old hotel. When I mentioned her to Owen, he informed me the hotel was well known as a brothel and casually speculated that she'd just come from an abortion in London.

As compared to our quick escape to the island that time, this visit Owen luxuriated in being a public figure again; I tagged along watching. His genuine pleasure at rehearsals, interviews, and at running into old friends on the street made me happy for him. But I was adrift again as I first was on the island, an awkward foreigner in constant need of guidance. The world observed me—the young American girl friend with notions about being a writer—and commented, "What's he doing with that child?" or, "What's a pretty young girl like her doing with him?" Our relationship was for the first time up for public comment, and I wasn't prepared for it, either by Owen or our life together up to now.

My naiveté makes me cringe. I had no sense of the scandal our relationship had caused in Owen's family and in certain circles of his friends. Wounded, I retreated, and was relieved to have found Catrina as a friend. She understands our life and Owen better than even I do—the anger and hurt behind his bold, swaggering front, his reputation as talented rebel, the city smiling with good cheer but secretly smirking, derisive but really jealous of our island life, waiting for a chance to stab him in the back. Protective, I was determined to get us out and back to the island as quickly as possible.

Immediately after opening night and the next day's reviews—mostly excellent, including a rave from Catrina—we rushed around town with the playwright's fee buying food and things to bring back to ease the coming season: bags of beans and rice, cans of juice, a small gas heater and a quilt, luxuries we've done without, a small surrender of the territory of abstinence. But we've proven our staying power, our ability to endure deprivations, and what are we trying to prove anyway? It is Harold's disapproving eye I see watching as we hoist our massive load into the train.

We reached Clochan in time to find Jack chugging away from the quay in crisp, cool sunlight. I was furious. We'd called ahead, left word we were on our way, but he'd gone without us. Had ten days away made us so insignificant? This is the unpredictability Jack is always assailed for. The barmaid said he'd be making a second run that night. So we'd just have to wait—all day in Clochan. Luckily it was a glorious day and the burden of the city quickly dropped away.

The West again! How reverentially the rest of the country utters those words, "The West"—Ireland's sacred coast. "Ah, *la dolce vita,*" friends had sighed as we escaped. "When are you ever going to get over it?" they jokingly complained, a little intolerant of our eyes still blurred with Celtic twilight.

The landscape in Clochan dizzied us as we strolled its peripheries looking for new views of the island which, mercifully, was still the shape we'd left it on the horizon. Our hearts rose. Jack returned at five and we sailed in at nightfall, lying on our backs alone on deck as the stars began to prick open the sky.

So many pleasures of the island have renewed themselves with departure and return. Today I begin to notice again things that had become the norm—like how much people touch here. A story's point is always punctuated with gesture—a hand on the shoulder or knee. Men throw their arms around each other without inhibition. Women often walk on the road arm in arm, or holding hands, though man and woman are never seen to.

There's but one notable exception to this physical camaraderie—an odd islander named Finbar. Tommy, delighted to have us back to propound to, and still in soaring spirits since the revival of his manhood, even though Maria is two weeks gone, gave a long hilarious tirade on this character Finbar in the West Village pub last night. "Another one of yur 'touch-me-nots'," he proclaimed. "Away in the head entirely."

Finbar is thin and wispish with hair so fair as to be nearly invisible. Instead of the characteristic cap, he wears a black vinyl hat with earflaps that a brother sent from America and a long muffler. He always walks with his arms crossed protectively over his chest and his eyes fixed on the ground. When we occasionally meet, he mumbles, "Not so bad" (of the day) and hurries squeamishly on.

"What's he hidin' from in that hat and scarf? Is it afraid of the fairies he is?" Tommy guffawed. " 'Tis a good job there is none of 'em left in this part of the world or it's himself they'd be after for shur—they know their own kind, that sort does."

Another man interjected, " 'Tis only close he is, Finbar," meaning reticent.

Then Tommy told this ridiculing story in a confiding stage whisper: Alone on the road late one night, drunk and veiled by the moonless dark, Finbar asked him what it was like to sleep with a woman (Tommy having the air of a man of great experience, apparently, in Finbar's vague eyes). He waited breathless for a reply. "Oh ye should try it, Finbar," Tommy leapt. "Ye'd sell all the cattle."

It's wonderful to be back in our lively enclave. But sadly, as predicted, Mrs. O'Malley died during our absence and it's fracturing to have missed her funeral. The end of an era. Her charge Seaneen went berserk for a night, committing some unspeakable desecration in the church (later revealed to have been his pissing on the altar). Now Seaneen has been taken in by a neighbor, and the archaic, quirky world of the post office is gone for good. The wife of Mrs. O'Malley's only nephew has already had the equipment moved and has set up shop in her own house, having long been prepared for her moment of glory. It's a bland, concrete-block room with a counter but no window slit, no smoke, no collection box for the chapel in Mayo, no stale cookies. All matter-of-fact, though shrill with gossip and complaints about the terrible state of the telephone line, and how did Mrs. O'Malley ever put up with it a'tall, because she won't.

Remarkable news in the mail: my book of poems, born and bred on the island, has been accepted by a London publisher. My excitement is matched by a swell of "rightness," a vindication of our being here. Owen too is beaming and strutting. The book is a pure product of this experience, and so it is a victory against all those who doubted my coming. It's a book I never could have written in the States—how long it would have taken me to find a comparably nourishing experience. How long I'd have floundered in my vague longings. My poems would have stayed dull, inward. This acceptance is a badge of verification I wish I'd had during our recent trip to Dublin—now I'm no longer merely aspirant.

Another remarkable event yesterday: the unannounced return of Mr. John Coyne, a brother of Theresa's, who left the island for the States as a young man, fifty-four years ago, and hadn't been back, or in touch, since. We saw his arrival on the quay as his head popped up out of the hold where he'd huddled during the rough crossing, his old face transformed to a child's as he took in the scene, every curve of the landscape as he'd left it, but the buildings unrecognizable. Where the hotel is now, he had worked for the last island landlord as a boy, that grand house now the concealed core of Catherine's empire. He stood staring, unable to decide on a move, or a response, or where he'd stay, or when and how he'd go introduce himself to a sister he hardly remembered. Our questions pressed him but yielded nothing. The whole quay was hopping with the drama of it, unwilling, even if he'd been capable of it, to let him move on. He asked after his old cronies, most dead, whose sons and grandsons and nephews surrounded him, eager for his memories and present impressions. We were eager too for his Rip Van Winkle observations. But Mr. Coyne was too flabbergasted to say much.

We waited among the crowd, hoping to glimpse the dramatic reunion with Theresa, but the crowd wouldn't let him go and soon ensconced him in the pub. He didn't seem in much of a hurry—having waited more than half a century and journeyed halfway around the world, he could afford to take his time.

Catherine told me the eventual climax this morning. Mr. Coyne finally climbed the hill, alone, at nightfall, climbed over the wall outside Theresa's house, and rapped on the front door—a sign of his Americanization. He heard mumbling, moving about, and knocked again. As those of us who know his sister could have predicted, the door stayed shut. He knocked once more.

"Who is it a'tall?" she shrieked.

"It's your brother," Mr. Coyne announced proudly.

Utter silence.

"Hello? Let me in," he insisted.

"I've no brother," she crackled, terror withering her vocal cords.

"What are you saying, of course you do, and he's standing right here."

"I've no brother. Only a brother in America and shur what would he be doin' here a'tall, he hasn't been heard of in fifty years or more."

"I'm the brother from America, woman!" He beat at the door in exasperation. To have come this far . . . "Now open the door, will you?"

She crept out the back door and around the side of the house to spy him while he kept up his hammer-

170

ing on the front door. He was her mirror-image. "Glory be to God," she gasped and fainted on the grass.

Later, revived, she brought him inside the house he'd left when she was a girl of three or four. He was a legend, hearsay, a man who'd lived in Pittsburgh all his adult life now picking his way through the bucket-and-basin disorder of her kitchen. She was beside herself. She ran down to Catherine's to buy bacon for his dinner and swore she'd never recover from the shock of it, never.

But today on the road she was glowing and declared him "a grand lad." He's to stay three weeks.

On dry days I walk in the afternoon. Dry days are intermittent now and almost always followed by rain. The clarity of the sky on an afternoon before rain is uncannily pellucid—faraway islands move forward as if the lens of the eye had been twirled. The air is perfectly still, the sea soundless. As always, I'm wafted into a dreamworld, but frequently interrupted now that I know every last person on the island. Mary O'Donnell, pining for her late husband, has parsley and kale to give me. What she really wants is conversation. I visit with her for an hour in exchange for a bag of vegetables—our mutual, implicit agreement—then continue my walk.

The last of the blackberries are withered along the crossroad. Nancy's and my laughing harvest there is gone without an echo—that season sleeps.

The days are shortening rapidly. Late afternoon drops precipitously into night. The light starts falling at four and soon will fall by three. By winter solstice, there will be but six hours of daylight—the inverse of summer's white nights. Life has already slowed down proportionally. The pub's half empty, the fields bare, house doors shut. Outdoor chores must be moved up to morning. Our schedule's shifted—we're boxed in by the dark.

And we've had our first wintry, three-day gale—wind battering the walls and windows, its blasts background to every breath. We move about silently, compulsively listening. No faraway romantically whistling howl, this, but direct impact. Wind so violent that it's said it will lift a sheep high enough into the air that its return fall will be fatal.

These stormy days seem endless, confined indoors. We wait it out, ears alert to the changing nuance of the wind. A storm never ends all at once. It teases us first—pauses, resumes. But when silence finally sticks, we somehow know for certain, and everyone in the village tentatively appears outside at the same moment greeting the calm and each other, calculating damage.

On the occasional calm day, we consult the experts to decide whether it's safe to go out in our curragh to catch a few fresh fish. They consult the sky and rattle off jingles:

> Mackerel skies and mares' tails
> Make tall ships shorten sails!

or,

> When the rain's before the wind
> Then your topsails you must mind;
> When the wind's before the rain
> Hoist your topsails up again!

Which side we are of the rain or wind is usually hard to ascertain, the two alternate so iambically. But most of the time we're too nervous to go out anyway, the sea quietly bittering.

Today it's dry and still. No one else on the road with me this afternoon as I walk. Another storm before morning's the word. In our village, smoke sluggishly rises vertically from the chimneys. Our own house, smokeless with absence, waits in the middle of the grey cluster.

The world's at bay and our own bailiwick is increasingly adequate again ("Thank God we're surrounded by water!"). After my unhappy experience of Dublin, I'm more sympathetic than before to Owen's tenacious clinging to the protection and grace of the island. He believes in the island as the sole answer to our needs and adjusts his behavior to it whenever necessary. His need to have the island as sanctuary makes him shy of risk, of possible offense to our neighbors. Owen's a much more cautious man now than the one I threw my life to the wind for. We arrived as outcasts but have moved steadily toward full acceptance.

Our passion for each other has become secondary to our passion for the way of life. Increasingly, though, I sense a contradiction between our daily life and the rhetoric of our life. Day to day I don't feel very radical, but much like a housewife doing double duty for lack of conveniences. My consolation is remembering that I'm living a life I couldn't have envisioned a few years back. Even if it's losing its luster with habit, I can imagine no comparably rich alternative.

But at the same time I'm disturbed by how inept I was in Dublin, how shattered I was when a friend of Owen's wife was introduced to me, turned her head, and refused to shake my outstretched hand. Perhaps my attraction to this shelter in truth has at its root a terror of the toughness of the world and a strong reluctance to adapt to and manage in it, though I didn't know

173

that when I came, and I'm not sure exactly what it is I'm afraid of.

The Clochan Players, a motley winter crew hungry for an audience, fought their way out to the island, costumes, props, and all, to perform Synge's *Playboy of the Western World*. Excited preparations erupted. Catrina is here visiting and delighted with the sudden spectacle. We watched all day as the old schoolhouse stage was cleared of stored turf, the high draughty windows patched with cardboard, and the floors swept and washed in preparation for the rare event. Every gaslight in the hall was lit come evening and the roads teemed with rain and traffic heading to the makeshift theater.

Wind was the leitmotif as the mouse-ravaged, mildewed curtain was ripped aside to reveal a stage set whose duplicate could be found in every kitchen on the island. On stumbled a huge Christy Mahon, straggle-haired, noisily gnawing on a raw carrot, the great "curiosity man," the smooth "mister honey," a man, despite his manure-stained jacket and graceless walk, who was indeed "fit to be holding his head high with the wonders of the world." Were I Pegeen—freckled, bold, and strapping, a descendant Grania Uaile would be proud of—I'd have fallen for him myself with his "poet's talking" and "bravery of heart" (a man out of the Tommy tradition). When he cried, "Oh, they're bloody liars in the naked parish where I grew a man," I glanced out the windows over at the barren mainland he'd come from and believed him. And I mourned along with Sarah Tansey—"You'd be ashamed this place, going up winter and summer with nothing worthwhile to confess at all." I was hearing Synge for the first time, knowing intimately the bitchy, desperate heart of the play.

Synge's lines sang true in the mouths of the Clochan Players. Who else but these wild Westerners could convincingly boast of a funeral, "There were five men, aye, and six men, stretched out retching speechless on the holy stones." And what other sort of Pegeen but a girl trapped for life in Clochan could sting our eyes as she wrenched out her final lament, "Oh, my grief, I've lost him surely. I've lost the only Playboy of the Western World." The gaslights went out on the stage and we were as lost and hopeless as she was. When the lights were relit, the Clochan Players laughed and bowed, delighted with themselves. We were delighted too. The confluence of play and players was thrilling. Catrina swore it was the greatest of the dozens of productions of the *Playboy* she'd seen in her career as a critic. "Far better than the last one at the Abbey," Owen punctuated smugly.

The contemporaneity of the play excited me—perhaps the West of Ireland is still in the "springtime" of its "local life" and an ideal home for a writer, as Synge believed in 1907 and we have come to believe. Synge feared its erosion even then, but given that his portrait of rural life is still so close to what we know here, it seems that life hasn't altered very much. This is still a place where it's worth putting your ear to the chink in the floor or wall as he did.

High from the excitement, we joined the Clochan Players in the pub for a celebratory toast. But surprisingly the islanders were not nearly as impressed as we were, knowing all the players in real life for what they were, and much too snobbish to think that people from Clochan could do justice to a play they'd heard the name of before. "They weren't suited to the parts," one sniffed. "The lad playin' Christy was like a monk," another. "They left out the music!" Even Sean: "That's a famous play, ye know. It deserves to be done better."

We looked at each other incredulously, suppressing our laughter while praising the Clochan production. The islanders are incurably insecure, always assuming that culture happens elsewhere.

It was a great charge, this performance, and wonderfully stimulating too to have Catrina here. Since Nancy left, she is the one woman I can really talk intimately with, the one who gives me perspective. She is also the only friend we have who can match Owen's wit and bring him down a notch. He lectures post-*Playboy:* "Every failure in love is due to a human limitation." Catrina, fresh from the breakup of a romance in Dublin, says, "Yeah, usually his." Owen goes on about the cleansing power of passion, the human and dramatic necessity of— "Give over, Owen," Catrina burbles, "Pegeen's just a bored lassie looking for a bit of excitement." "Exactly!" Owen resumes. But Catrina challenges his dominating charisma with her own. She has, funnily enough, taught me how to talk to him and hold my own.

That autumn there wasn't much free-lance work and we were so poor that we had to borrow ten pounds at a time from a number of Owen's friends. Amazingly, gifts of money arrived in the mail—the community of writers helping out without moral judgment about Owen's position, unquestioningly loyal to a fellow member of the profession. Or so Owen pontificated about it, as if it were frequent and normal among them; he said he'd helped out others when he had money, and would again. But I suffered over these "loans," finding myself in humiliating gratitude to people I hardly knew, or in some cases disliked, trapped in a web of social obligations and public knowledge of our hardship. They came to visit and we would have to visit them. I could barely scrape together decent meals and endured their silent discomfort.

Once we found ourselves completely cleaned out, without even enough pennies to buy a stamp to write a letter to someone to ask for money. We waited out the mail in hopes there'd be a check in it. For four days a gale blew and we rationed our remaining food till it couldn't be rationed to stretch any longer. On the fifth day, foodless, the gale still blew. Owen marched us off to the East Village and into Bridget's to ask for groceries on credit. She never blinked an eye, but gave me a little red notebook to write down what we'd bought and refused to check the list or sums herself but said we could pay it off in a chunk whenever we wanted. (From then on we lived with that arrangement, and she argued with me every time I gave her a check that we couldn't possibly owe so much.)

Owen, though vociferously grateful, always felt we deserved the help we got, that our position was unimpeachable; I never felt anything other than guilt and terror. For Owen it was part of the price and privilege of being a writer. But in my worry I wondered if we deserved such exceptional status. If I thought no, I couldn't think so for long because I had no way to alter the situation. With Owen and the island I had chosen extreme financial insecurity and lack of opportunity, and now I was trapped in it. Owen had no intention of getting permanent work, and there was no job for me to go out and get unless I left the island, the country, and him. So his choices had to be mine if I wanted to stay—and I did. And all his choices were made to keep us on the island and writing, at any cost. Well, I'd learned to be a writer anyway. I'd learned to write hard all day because there was little else to do and it kept my mind off worry. We went out less often to the pub as taxes skyrocketed and drink got too expensive, stayed home most nights reading. I read long Russian novels and did not feel sorry for myself—one had to feel a virtuous sense of mission in order not to feel despair or self-pity, and that edge was what kept us going when things did not improve much that year or the one after.

Catrina writes charmingly: "Cheer up, the worst is definitely over. As for money, none of us will ever have the rude stuff, and the sooner the bank managers wise up to that the better it will be for their ulcers. Take a firm line with yours, make explanations about dark 'personal emergencies' and promise to pay him back by next summer, saying that you are quite willing to pay interest. Point out, if it seems necessary, that this is what banks are in business for, the lending of money. Stand no nonsense!"

While we hid inside from gales all week, major events have taken place—scandals—now the only subject of conversation as the winds abate and life resumes on the roads.

Tommy has received word, frantic, no doubt, that the object of his summer fling is pregnant! He is a touching mixture of pride and bewilderment. Of course he and Maria must marry—in this society there is no alternative. Official reaction is hushed and condemning. But unofficially, there's amusement and glee for Tommy. And of course we are delighted at this turn in his fate, what it will mean for him. The worry is if they can make the marriage work, these two oddballs. He is leaving for London tomorrow and will look for a job, any kind of a job, living, meanwhile, in Maria's father's house. A big adjustment for him, but from a reservoir inside him there's risen a confident readiness for what may come. Maria dotes on him, and Tommy finally will have something to work for, something to believe in.

Tommy's departure from the island will leave a large, audible gap. His send-off tonight, after hours of drinking and joking, was tearful all around. Everyone, even his casual enemies, came back from Richard's to join the wake at the West Village pub. And the talk was wild, pent up for days. It's there we heard what else has been going on all week.

Brendan and Agnes apparently arrived here from Boar two weeks ago, at Brendan's insistence, for the winter. But Brendan had been in Boar all summer so had made no preparations for winter here—he had cut no turf. He borrowed a few sacks when they arrived at their cold, mildewed house, and looked into buying some. Meanwhile, while he was back at the pub the other afternoon, the turf ran out and Agnes, out of either spite or stupidity, threw an old tractor tire on the last of the sods. A huge fire erupted and sent flames high up through the chimney. The whole village ran out and Agnes fled the house, hysterical. Bridget's son beat the fire out with a blanket. Gossip says Agnes has gone mad and this proves it, but, on the other hand, "What kind of a man leaves a woman and two babies in a storm with no turf for the fire?" Conjecture is they'll soon return to the warmth of her father's house on Boar.

More scandalous and hushed than even Tommy's misdemeanor has been an "incident" between Maura and Will. Those more attuned than ourselves have long known that something was going on there. That nightly 3:00 A.M. ride over from the West Village pub Maura makes is not without a passenger. One morning, up before dawn to go cockling, Owen had seen the car parked in a hidden corner of the beach.

They were found together in a barn. To protect herself and her marriage, Maura is claiming Will attacked her. She's produced a pair of broken glasses to prove it. Will, glumly, is taking the rap. Maura, fervent, has called in the police from the mainland and demanded the price of a new pair of glasses.

It is fascinating, but disheartening, to see how the community is handling this sexual indiscretion. Will has to leave—he will go to England before the police officer comes in on the boat Tuesday morning to question him.

Two young island men to be lost to England, one needlessly. I am sad for Will, who didn't choose to go to England like his older brothers but wanted to stay on the island. "That woman needs a kick in the arse," Sean complains righteously. "It's two kicks she needs, one in each arse," another man chimes in, momentarily softening Sean. But his sense of injustice is sharp: "It's herself should be goin', not the poor laddie."

The gossip's been pitiless, but Maura's still resi-

dent in the pub, piously showing face, an innocent,
though the pressure's thinned her skin. She lashed out
finally in a delicious ruction with Baby Chop who had
sidled into the pub on tiptoe to buy herself a drop of
whiskey for a toothache. Simultaneously, a brother of
Will's came by to pick up the melodeon and walked
ostentatiously through the pub with it in its case, glar-
ing at Maura on the way out. Baby Chop piped up at
the sight of the melodeon case: "What's that a'tall? It
has the look of a doctor's case to it."

Ripe for innuendo, Maura snapped back, "What
business is it of yurs anyways?"

Baby Chop, well known for non sequiturs, came
back, "And didn't yur grandmother go round wearin'
her scarf like this over her face?" She pulled hers down
till it covered her nose and stood there gesticulating
blindly.

Maura leapt up, livid. "At least that way she
couldn't be lookin' into other people's business." Then
she set on Baby Chop tooth and nail, ripping the kerchief from her face, leaving her denuded, squawking,
the pub in alarums.

Sean boldly intervened and separated the pair.
Maura was subdued by the nervous crowd ("It's only
playactin' she is yet," a man predicted) while Baby
Chop, shaken, ran out protesting, "She'd bite the head
off of ye for a joke, God help us, she would so."

After a few philosophical sighs, the incident
vanished from the room—the repressions of propriety.
But of course it is already legended, already a chapter
in the island's continuously accumulating oral history.
All these incidents are. Tommy is a hero among bachelors, the man who deflowered a nun. Agnes has earned
her spot as the wicked witch of the west, or a "poor
unfortunate woman," depending on whom you're talk-

ing to. And the West Village pub is minus two men and a melodeon.

Michael Hammers has been sent out to the hospital in Galway. Catherine knew it was bad, and word has come back that he's dying of bone cancer. The island is shocked—he is such a lively, happy, and healthy-seeming man, one of the best. Sean is especially devastated—Michael is one of his closest friends.

In the East Village I see his bicycle propped up against the window in the porch of his smokeless house and it feels, though he's in some limbo in Galway, as if he's already dead, another islander and house lost. We are depressed and frustrated by the unreality of it. Many of the most important events in an islander's life take place off the island—birth, education, illness, death. The town of Galway, sixty miles away, rends the islanders apart at so many crucial junctures.

Firmly setting his jaw, Sean hired a taxi from Clochan to Galway to visit Michael Hammers. He found him palely staring out a window at a gas station on the street below—his only view from the hospital room—his hands emptily turned up by his sides. Michael couldn't believe Sean had come so far to see him and burst into tears. He cried that the next time he'd be on the island it would be in a coffin, and Sean said, "Stop talkin' nonsense," but Michael said, "It's a queer thing, thinkin' of the island goin' on without me," and Sean said the island'd never be the same without him, and finally Sean yielded and cried too, and Michael held onto his hand as he was leaving to catch the boat and said, "For God's sake tell Catherine I'll be happier dyin'

182

on the island near my friends and brothers and to get
me the hell out of this place."

But she couldn't.

I remarked to Catherine how sleepy we've been of late,
often going to bed by ten. All the stormy days confined
inside perhaps. She asked what we'd been eating. We've
been short of fresh vegetables, our yield very low this
year, and when I told her so, she tsk-tsked and went into
her pantry for a big bag of carrots. She said we were
probably vitamin deficient and carrots were the thing.

Sure enough. After a dinnerplateful of them we
were up till one in the morning, lively as the rabbits
who plundered them in the garden all summer. This
morning I called the pharmacy in Clifden to send in a
month's supply of vitamins.

But the incident upset me. "Deficiency" is part
of a vocabulary remote from my former life. I hadn't
thought of the long-term effect of our limited diet.
We'd arrived without foresight or a great deal of prac-
ticality. We'd only meant to live cheaply, out of the
workaday world. I hadn't meant to suffer. Or perhaps
secretly I did, in atonement for early comforts. But
suffering is no longer any contribution to sensibility; it
is only a hindrance. All I gain from it now is a sad
identification with my neighbors.

How much do the islanders suffer? I have tended
to take their physical and psychic afflictions at face
value, as defining, rather than measuring them against
a standard of health. From the start I thought of them
as unalterable, fixed in a pattern tied to the culture.
But in the December dark I see the abyss at the center

of the island psyche and wonder at its inevitability. Half the children are out of school with the flu. Posture and gait have altered to a huddle, and a wince is setting its lines into damp faces.

From the top of the hill, the vista looks bleak—so different from the island I first fell in love with. The fields are made of curds of mud, the sea and sky and rock share a single shade of grey. Seabirds screech with a cold, hysterical edge in their voices. The mail boat goes out, but instead of sketching a straight diagonal across the channel, it tosses, veers, rises, falls. "Ye won't see anymore now till winter," a man on the road prophesies—meaning, winter's almost upon us. "This place is no use a'tall in winter."

Autumn and winter are the only times one hears islanders reacting to the landscape. They are indifferent all spring and summer while I ogle. The extraordinary beauty of the island and its setting mean little to them. But the depredations of autumn bring ready comment—the messiness of the roads, the messiness of the days, the dull lumpiness of the hills relieved only by a smattering of auburn heather.

It's the same with Harold—his responses have become an islander's. He's broody, short-tempered, solitary, insulated from attachments or pleasures. He drinks till closing time with his few West Village buddies, then sleeps away half the day, barely managing his own survival, not to speak of doing any painting. His identification with his neighbors has become so complete that he's even been going to mass though he's been vociferously anticlerical all his life. Harold has bonded himself to the bitterest part of island life and is going down with it. We have no more in common with him now than with any other islander.

That bonding and submergence is the great risk

in a place like this. The arena is so small and compelling that it's easy and convenient to conform. For
those like me, desperate to belong to a place and to feel
rooted, the danger is greatest. Lacking a solid sense of
self when I arrived, I have let the island penetrate my
deepest being. It has given me the identity I lacked at
home, replaced home. Only my sense of myself as writer
has held me back from complete absorption by the
island. It's Harold's loss of himself as artist that's allowed him to plunge in over his head.

It's a seductive plunge. When an old woman in
Clifden, hearing my accent, said, "Yur not from around
these parts, are ye?" I said, "No." "Don't tell me"—she
closed her eyes and held out her hand like a diviner.
"I'll guess. Yur from Donegal." I couldn't have been
more delighted. Friends say I even look Irish now. The
gap in my personality must have been very large to have
accommodated such a transforming invasion.

It would take being elsewhere, off the island, to
test how truly this world defines me now. But Owen
wouldn't want to try that. To go back to the States
would force us to compromise with a society we both
find repugnant. "You'd never make the readjustment,"
Nancy wrote recently, bored with law school and the
life she and Rick have had to fall into. Owen and I
may, by now, be like those horses taken off the island
on the boat who would, to quote myself, "never walk
the same on mainland."

But I'm forced to look at our life here honestly.
Our adventure has, I'm afraid, rigidified—first into a
series of habits, and now into a dogma. Owen in many
ways is as confined by his new philosophy of freedom
as he was by the traditional straitjacketed upbringing
that he rebelled against originally. He will, I'm afraid,
be stuck forever preaching the religion that changed

his life and never venture on to anything new again. He wouldn't like to hear that. I've never said it. To me, he says gratefully, "You gave me back my madness."

When I'm depressed he panics at my discontent—we've seldom fought, have always been easygoing and harmonious. So he cannot be reasonable or balanced now, but automatically assumes my glumness means I'll leave—the island, him. What's an urge in me, as yet unclear, he pushes immediately to debate. It comes down to the question of how you are going to live your life, he says, and won't allow me the greys of other options. He is alarmed, confused, but then so am I.

This turmoil has colored everything, especially my writing. My poems have become inward and abstract again, no longer fed by the life around me. They've become nebulous to me because there is no one to listen, no one to talk back—except Owen, who can't any longer read them with an honest eye. I put them in envelopes and send them to American magazines. Six months later they return in print. Whom have I spoken to or for? I can write publishable poems now, but I have no source of new ideas, no means of testing myself. I lack a community of peers. I've lost incentive. Some days I just read the dictionary, accumulate words I haven't yet found a vehicle for.

We have holed up for winter. The windows are sealed with masking tape; we've hung blankets over the doors and blocked off their bottoms with burlap sacks. There's a reassuring stack of turf against the gable of the house and a fifty-pound sack of flour sent in from Clifden. The storms challenge our steadfastness with their severity and enforced confinement. This week, a five-day blow, gale force eight for most of it, some gusts breaking ninety miles per hour. Yeats's "haystack-and-roof-levelling wind bred on the Atlantic."

Rain slams the windows in slabs, bowlfuls spilling from the sill. My reflection breaks apart in the glass. Three new leaks have sprung in the kitchen and we have pots and basins beneath to catch them. Drip, boom, drip, boom. Or sometimes, momentarily, it's oddly quiet and I feel as if we're in a vacuum, the pressure about to collapse on us.

Only talk in the pub can relieve the weight of these identical, beset days. But the talk comes less frequently, reluctantly, buried too deeply under gloom. When it does come, it comes manically: they joke about the winter solstice—"It'll all be better after the turn of the day. Shur, after the turn of the day, even the cock's step is an inch longer." "Is that true?" I ask gullibly. "Shur, that's the God's honest truth, isn't it Pat, the step of the cock bein' an inch longer." And they all get in a laugh at my expense.

The talk, when it's roused, is also reminiscential, harkening back to those now unimaginable days of late summer. Sean retells all the summer's tales, cementing them into history, clinging fervently to those last bright images in the face of the dark and the wind.

"Do you remember," he begins, "the night Rick came in here after fishin', complainin' how tired he was . . . he was a grand lad the same Rick, wasn't he? Well he made me laugh. Ye Yanks always sayin' 'How ya doin'?' and I'd had my bellyful of bein' asked 'How ya doin'?' by every Yank that ever came to this island, and so in walks Rick and he says, 'How ya doin' Sean?' and I says, 'Well, I couldn't be doin' worse, Rick, I hadn't a wink of sleep since Sunday,' and this was a Wednesday we were talkin' on. 'I hadn't a wink of sleep since Sunday with this turf to save, and every time I try to get a bit of a rest in the mornin' doesn't this curse of a donkey of mine come roarin' over to the window the moment the sun comes up. The divil! And so up I am again and off to the bog, no sense tryin' to sleep with that rascal at ye. I'll be kilt altogether, I swear it!' So I'm tellin' this to poor Rick, who's tired himself, the crature, and he's lookin' very thoughtful like and he says, 'You could put a blindfold on the donkey so he doesn't wake up so early.' Well, I nearly died. A blindfold on a donkey? Couldn't ye see them staggerin' round the road with kerchiefs tied round their heads! 'Well,' I says, 'yur too much altogether, ye Yanks. Ye have an answer for everything, don't ye's? Well, more power to ye, good luck to ye then, but don't go blindfoldin' any donkey of mine, thanks very much.' So Rick says, 'But I thought you wanted to find a way to sleep in the morning.' So I says to him, 'Arra, they'll be plenty of time for sleepin' in the winter,' and isn't that the God's honest truth too. So Rick starts laughin'. 'I don't understand you, Sean,' he says. 'When I asked you how you were, you said you were bad.' Then I says, 'Bad? Shur, ye haven't seen bad yet, Rick, shur ye haven't. Ye just wait around a few more months if it's bad yur lookin' for.' And he should've too. He was a grand lad. So anyways, he says, 'Have a drink, Sean,' and I says, 'I wouldn't mind if I did, Rick,' so he shouts over to Richard for two double whiskeys, doubles, mind ye, and he puts a five-pound note down on the counter to pay for 'em. He was a grand lad that Rick, and his wife too, she was a grand lassie. Well it's too bad the pair of 'em isn't in it right now and we'd see how hard they are a'tall because it takes a hard man to stick a winter on this island."

" 'Tis true enough," the other men pipe up, looking around at the diminished population, then all staring at their boots as Sean concludes sourly: "Aren't I tellin' ye's the truth? This place is worthless in the winter. Shur, that Canadian lad that rented the Cunnane house, ye didn't see till he was takin' off, makin' out it was a book he was writin', the chancer! One good gale put the fear of God in 'im. And sure poor John Coyne, he's gone now too, the poor maneen. He was lonesome to be goin' too, and Theresa's lonesome after him. But didn't he say he'd be comin' back to stay for good, after all those years in America, could ye credit it? That's what he promised Theresa, she told me so herself. Well, we'll see now, we'll see about that . . ."

The Last Winter

The north wind gives me no rest, and death is in the sky.

—Traditional song

December 17: Bad gales in showers. No boat.
December 18: Wicked night—southwest gales force nine to ten and cold. Moderating during day to force seven to eight. No boat.

December 19: Southwest gales. No boat.

December 20: Southwest gales. No boat.

December 21: Southwest gales. No boat.

December 22: Southerly gales. No boat.

December 23: Southerly gales. No boat. A government helicopter brings in doctor and medical supplies and several schoolchildren stranded on the mainland.

December 24: Westerly winds, force five to seven, sea still wild, but as it's Christmas Eve, Jack goes out, with a crew of fifteen as ballast and help, and brings in food, mail, and whiskey for Christmas. A triumph!

December 25: Christmas Day. Southerly gales. No boat.

December 26: Saint Stephen's Day. Southerly gales. No boat.

December 27: South to southwest gales. No boat.

December 28: Beginning to moderate, sea still up. No boat.

Winter solstice came and went without any noticeable difference in the stride of roosters. On the mainland, druids gathered at ancient tumuli to witness the sun's once-yearly illumination of burial chambers at the end of winding passageways. A flock of wild geese, wintering on the Gentle Island, whirred overhead, pointing. No one's the wiser, but the long nights imperceptibly begin to surrender, a few seconds today, a few seconds tomorrow.

Christmas was unregardingly dark and stormy, an extremity of abuse I doubted the island could rise above. Neighbors waited until after the startling swoop of the helicopter (which we'd fantasized over for days, having heard on the radio that Tory Island off Donegal had been rescued and wondering why not us, why not us) waited till Christmas Eve itself to spruce up their houses, even painting at the last minute so that the rooms still reeked and the walls couldn't be touched when we went to call with gifts of cake and whiskey at nightfall. Huge fires, twice as turf-rich as usual, were molded in the hearths, veritable pyramids; freshly washed hair glimmered in the soft light. Well, nothing can put a dent in Christmas, with the children home from boarding school and hams finally brought in from the mainland and stacks of breads and cakes cooling. Even the weeks just past with hardly a boat and the unceasing misery of the driven rain couldn't dent it, and the miraculous run of the boat that afternoon made us nearly levitate with sense of occasion.

There was so much Christmas mail on the boat, finally in at three, that Sean the Post didn't make it to our door till 10:30 that night, reeling from the glass of whiskey he'd had to drink at each house, his Christmas tip. He was burdened with packages from America and packages from England and bundles of cards, and he swayed in our kitchen drinking yet another glass of whiskey, sorting through the village pile plump with letters and cards for us, and swearing it'd be Christmas morning itself till he was finished "distributin' the post." Forty-eight letters and Christmas cards had accumulated for us, including one from Sean which, ridiculously, had gone out to Clochan to be sorted, stranded, then brought back in, with my name touchingly Gaelicized to "Debagh."

Candles glowed in every window of every lived-in house on the island. It's at Christmas that an abandoned house is most disheartening. Rosie says that in the years before we came, they'd always come up to light Christmas candles in the empty house anyway, for the neighbors' sake.

A new priest is here to celebrate Christmas mass. And surprisingly, a priest of a wholly different sort than the previous baby-faced one who with his squeamish propriety and parochial intransigencies would not speak to us. To befriend us would have meant to condone our status. The most controversial thing the former priest managed to do was to let sheep into the graveyard one summer to trim the grass. Though most regarded him as weak, they still altered their voices for the reverential "Father," and none defied him.

The new priest is young—this is his first assignment—he has an open mind and a real education, and he is befriending the islanders on his own terms, including us. Already he's come by to borrow books and talk about Merton and Zen. The islanders are guarded. They're used to iron-handed, inscrutable leaders. The priest rules every realm of island life: he's moral and political arbiter, controller of education and entertainment, psychiatrist, lawyer, direct representative of God. The entire bureaucracy of the island resides in his single being. He is treated lavishly, given food and turf. His house is kept painted and dry, his garden lush. His house, in fact, is hidden from the road by a jungle of bushes, and the only two trees on the island flank his walk—a pair of palms warmed by Gulf Stream currents and protected from the battering wind by a hillock and the southwest wall of the church. The house is white and square and is graced with large picture windows, unthinkable in an exposed spot, but here opening onto views of the yard's rich sun-trap foliage.

We've only just become privy to this house and garden because of our warm acquaintance with the new priest. He's been more successful with Catherine and us than with his more typical parishioners. Perhaps he isn't politic enough for a place like this. The islanders suspect his openness, his unwillingness to direct every facet of their lives. Already he finds their back-stabbing wearying and is somewhat bewildered by the reality of his mission as opposed to his pure idea of it.

Christmas Day, Catherine climbed the hill with four bottles of wine for us, three of which she'd received instructions to send up in phone calls from friends in Dublin, including Catrina, and one a gift from herself. Bounty made holiday—Nouveau Beaujolais, cheese and crackers, and a fire roaring with a specially saved log.

The next day, Stephen's Day, the children went pagan and mad, roaming the island in gangs, bursting in doors unannounced, masked, painted, bedraggled, piping, dancing, and singing at the top of their lungs in their ritual "hunting of the wren." Cookies and pennies buy off their shrieks, the players curtsy and bow, then streak out through the rain to their next stage, indefatigable.

The Last Winter

Once Christmas is past and the shock of the coming months of unvarying gloom hits, 'tis the season to hibernate, to stare tranced into the fire, to do as little as possible. Rousing themselves to believe that summer will eventually return, some men mend nets, prepare fishing gear. Sean's uncle, the survivor Sean Ginger, nightly stretches his trammels in the oil-light before Rosie's hearth to inspect and stitch, casting tangled shadows on the far wall. Rosie and Ann sit glumly in front of the fire as if it were the center of the universe. Blankly, they wait for bedtime, or for callers like ourselves to interrupt their aimless meditations, Sean Ginger's snail's-pace work, and what Robin Flower aptly describes as "the intermitted talk."

Once interrupted, Sean Ginger stops and carves a plug of tobacco for his pipe, smokes and squints. He surveys his net with its history of terror and fecundity written in gaps and patches, and talks, inevitably, of the old days, when the island was in "the elements of its glory," when the men could hardly be held back from fishing at nightfall, and even in winter would seize a good day whenever it came, and when it didn't they'd gather winkles and searods on the strand instead (the latter to be sold on the mainland for boiling down and extracting iodine). "The old ones—those were the people now. This new crowd, shur . . . they're afraid to put a foot in the tide. Isn't it a queer thing?" He pokes at a tear in his net. "A mullet did that. 'Tis a job itself now to catch the mullet—the mullet is as cute (meaning crafty), right in and out with him, no delayin' in the net for that fellow." He takes up mending the hole the mullet made and the kitchen settles itself with sighs. Well, he's right, the old ones are the people—who have the patience, the lore, the drive to remember and keep up the large story of themselves. The young boys in the pub have lost the art of net-mending and thatch-making and a lot of other arts. They are clever with boat and car engines and building with concrete blocks instead of stones. What's distinct to islanders is diluted in them. The world has changed them, and they will change the island.

In the older people I watch the remains of a great tradition, a resourcefulness older than Grania Uaile. And I cling to the colors and rituals of that tradition because it's given me so much faith and pleasure, and because I hope the young here won't have to grow up with the crassness and wishy-washy conformities I was reared on.

The children are wild about television. One household has bought a set which it runs off car batteries, the batteries periodically recharged off Richard and Catherine's generator. The children flock to this house every evening their parents will let them flee homework and chores to watch *Kojak* and *Rhoda* and *Hawaii Five-O*. They don't understand the accents or the jokes or the world these characters live in, but they begin to use them as a standard—of life and of entertainment. Will they ever be content to stay on the island? Children I meet try to impress me with the extent of their knowledge of things American and look hungrily for more. "Is it true, Deba, in New York that people get kilt every day, more people than in Belfast altogether? That's what the schoolmaster said, but shur what does he know, he was never in it himself like ye were." I tell them it's true. "Then why would anyone want to live there a'tall?" A good question. I tell them that's why I'm living here. "Shur, there's nothin' to do here," they shrug.

So many signs of modern life have shown up since we arrived five years ago. At least ten cars and a number of tractors and dumpers now navigate the stony roads. The island had its first traffic accident, fortunately minor. There's more prosperity in evidence, more stylishness. There was even, ludicrously, a Tupperware party the other night! I couldn't believe my ears when Bridget said she hoped I'd be there. A representative from the mainland came in to explain the wonders of air-tight plastic and all the women gazed at me, a veteran of plastic, for a signal—would I support the flag, lead the way with purchases? Reluctantly, with moldy bread in mind, and their lust for progress pressing me, I did. The women cooed and committed themselves to pounds' worth; by the next week the island's bread was being stored in big rectangular plastic boxes instead of in tea towels in the dresser and everyone was singing anthems to plastic. We can't figure out where they get the money for it all, even with the increases in the dole and enlarged agricultural grants. Many of them have surpassed us in comforts, and we feel somewhat left behind by this little boom propelling the island toward the late twentieth century. We're poor even by island standards now.

Though I mourn these changes, I'm more understanding of them than before. Knowing hardship as they do, aren't they right to eliminate it wherever they can? They can't be blamed for wanting washing machines and freezers. They'll leave and get them elsewhere if they can't get them here. But I'm too keenly aware of the economic tyranny of the world of conveniences, which I feel such freedom in the absence of, and which they feel so deprived, lacking. I worry how much the island must change in order to survive, remain populated.

I live here and try to become a part of what's passing. I move backward as they move forward. My every act is a choice, a contribution toward the large weft I want to see strengthened, the fabric of island culture I hope will hold despite their self-destructive wishes.

A palm reader visited and sat before the fire. She was a friend of a friend who had sent her to call on us. She was French, black-haired, and small, and moved as lightly as Ariel. We drank the brandy she'd brought as a gift and her eyes intensified in the firelight. She asked could she have a piece of turf to bring back to Paris to keep in her flat. Turf has mysterious powers, she said.

She read our palms, and holding my hand in hers looked at me searchingly, gauging. "Shall I tell you the truth?" she asked quietly.

"Of course."

She spoke so softly Owen couldn't hear. "Your fate line is broken and only your own daring will re-join it. You will soon have to cross a battlefield and a new line will eclipse this old one. It will be precarious. You must be careful. You are like a three-legged table, and Owen is the fourth leg. But the table must learn to balance itself on three legs alone."

Theresa flies in to gossip: wood sighted on shore ("Ye run down to it Owen"), and as if in afterthought, "Gerald and Mary'll be gettin' married now."

"Oh, how marvelous." A lovely young island couple who since late summer have been seen together in the pub, she causing a small sensation as the first young woman to be so daring, drinking and carrying on a courtship in public. I was delighted that two young people had decided to stay, to tie their lives to the island's and make a go of it, though they'd be on the dole and need to find a house.

But Theresa muttered to herself in displeasure.

"What, aren't people happy about it?" I asked.

"Shezezptn," Theresa garbled.

"What?"

"She's expectin'." Theresa looked away and forced the ugly words out of herself.

So that was it, they were getting married because she'd gotten pregnant, and it wouldn't be forgotten or forgiven, it would hardly count as a real marriage. Just proves what happens when you let women into the pub—I could hear it all. It was okay for me to drink in the pub, except that it inspired people like Mary. None of the island's flexibility and openness with outsiders applies to their own. But apparently plenty of island women have managed to get pregnant before their weddings in the past without the aid of alcohol, so I don't know what all the fuss is about.

In the past few days the island has rigidified into official joylessness about the marriage. Quite different from the amused response to Tommy's forced marriage, the fallen woman being a non-islander in that case. There is also, apparently, "class" snobbery at work, Gerald's family regarding itself as part of a higher echelon of island life than Mary's. It's hard to imagine that such social distinctions exist given the fact that they're all on the dole, and except for the most miserable bachelors, all live in fairly identical houses, eat identical food, and wear identical clothing. But there is family history to be measured, the reputations of ancestors, and the perceived economic status of how much and what land is owned, number of cows, etc. That Gerald's family thinks he is marrying beneath himself is rather comic to us though.

Watching the island's worst narrowmindedness in action has so annoyed me that I'm helping to make sure this will be a happy wedding. Mary was one of Catherine's kitchen staff last summer, so out of loyalty, Catherine is making a party in the hotel and I'm helping with the preparations.

The greatest problem, though, that Mary and Gerald face is that they can't find a house to live in, and neither set of parents is willing to take them in, even temporarily. They were hoping to rent a house until they could afford to build one of their own. But with this wish they fell into a morass. Because of us and Harold and summer tourists who fight over the few comfortable available houses, there is a good deal of money to be made by renting out a house. The value of these cold, damp houses has been ridiculously inflated by their scarcity and the growing demand. And so no one is willing to sacrifice income by renting to an island couple who can't, even on a year-round basis, match what's made on summer rentals.

When finally there are two people courageous enough to be forthright, and to want to remain islanders, not exiles in England as they would likely have become in the past in these hostile circumstances, everything in the community is geared to shut them out.

Twice the wedding has been postponed because of the house dilemma, for me a source of fury and guilt (Rosie, I feel it likely, would have offered them this house were we not in it, her compassion being greater than her greed). But finally, a solution has been devised, unique to the island, clever, but unfortunate. They have borrowed the money to buy a trailer, here called a "caravan," a metal rectangle with fold-away tables and beds, a little gas stove and heater (no hearth, what a house's center is). In this box, plopped down on a scrap of field outside the village, they'll make some sort of home for themselves. Of course there's mockery and anger about the purchase of the caravan, it having short-circuited the little drama so many were delighting in. And some, including Catherine, are upset about the blight it will cause (the tourists must be considered), this excuse for a house brought in from the industrial mainland. As sad as the whole episode has been, and uncomforting as life will be in that metal corridor, its purchase is an important gesture toward the island's future survival. Things must change, the island must be grateful to those willing to continue populating it, and adapt to their needs. If they won't be given houses, they'll have to bring in their own, in whatever form.

The wedding is on for tomorrow, and until the caravan arrives, Mary and Gerald will be staying with an elderly bachelor uncle of hers who has a crumbling house up here at the top of the hill.

This fortnight of drama has sparked me to life, made me feel more myself, who I was on arrival, an outcast too. I feel rebellious again, want the islanders to know us for what we really are rather than the acceptable couple we've adapted ourselves into. With this feeling has come an increasing itch to get out, to be elsewhere, at least for short periods. My closeness now to Catrina, and the stimulation of some of the people we've met in town through her, has become more alluring. Painters, writers, theater people, IRA proselytizers— a belligerent, lively crowd with the gumption and intelligence we're often deprived of here. With both desire for that contact and financial need as motivations, I've talked Owen into taking on more radio and television writing work in the past year, which necessitates our often traveling to Dublin. We stay with Catrina when in town and fill ourselves with food and talk and plays and films and arrive back ready to face our harsh solitude again.

The Last Winter

Owen sometimes goes on his own while I stay home to write—our first separations in all these years. I thought I couldn't manage here without him, in the most basic sense: I can't make it up the steep hill with the big bucket of water from the well. But I had to laugh when I devised an obvious solution—why not carry half a bucket up twice a day instead?

While I'm here alone, Owen and Catrina both write to me daily. Owen senses the significance of the transition we're going through and though his principles of freedom should dictate an openness toward my new independence, he is afraid. "Don't work too hard," he writes as I try to finish a group of new poems. "Bolt the door at night." And, "Some small part of you (but how large?) must be intensely relieved to have me off your back—at last." Though quaking, he's courageously begun to confront my frustrations. "Go ahead. Demand the moon. I trust we will come through this intact."

Catrina reports: *"The Irish Times* is here in the kitchen interviewing Owen about the life of the writer in the West and he is telling them about thrift stores and the lessons to be learned from walking in dead men's shoes! How *do* you put up with him?!"

She says, "It's touching how deeply he loves you, and what you've made possible for him. But with all his talk about freedom, doesn't he sometimes forget about yours?"

"What's freedom for?" Theodore Roethke wrote. "To know eternity." I long to know more—the cities of Europe, other people, other worlds. It took freedom to come here. And it will take freedom to leave.

Along with the crucial emotional risks of these new arrangements, the practical problem of going in and out to Dublin has become the bane of our existence. Stranded on the island by storms, I remember Jack's gloomy mumbling—"Islands are fine places, yes sir, till ye want to get off 'em." We fire off telegrams to the city canceling all appointments, slip books out of suitcases, food out of plastic bags, and sit paralyzed by the fire waiting for a break. As the weather changes, Jack equivocates, waits for the turn of the tide, holds us in limbo. "An island is a ship without sails," a man in the pub ruminates, pitying us.

Even worse is being stranded off the island. We might call from Dublin on a perfectly fine day to hear the new postmistress whine, "It's blowin' a gale here." It's hard to know whether to trust her pessimism and stay on in the warmth of Catrina's house, or to race across the country, two hundred miles, on a positive hunch and then be stopped at the edge of the sea, unable to go the last stretch, seven miles to home. Frustrated, we backtrack, go to friends in Clifden in view of the sea, watch, wait, and remember Ann's bitter forecast that the vagaries of the boat would be "the death of ye's."

One night, desperate to get back in to the island, we discovered that Jack hadn't come out, but two fishing boats had, owned by each of two brothers who hadn't spoken in twenty years or more. We're closer to Martin than Pat, so loaded our things in his wheelhouse, grateful for the passage, had a few drinks with him in the pub, and set out in the dark.

The night wasn't good—a big roll in the sea and spatterings of wind like a sudden cat-o'-nine-tails. My heart fluttered wondering about Jack's decision not to sail—I've always respected his instincts and caution. Also, Martin had been drinking even before we arrived (Jack never touches a drop), and the boat is a small, motorized lobster boat bought through a government grant program and often mocked—the wrong shape for these waters. The boat smacked itself against each oncoming wave, jarring my insides. Martin's brother's boat was ten minutes behind us, a vague light disappearing and rising and disappearing.

Halfway into the channel, as if my secret fears had nursed events to life, the motor grunted and sputtered and then fell silent. Martin cursed. Sickeningly, the engine turned round and round without catching as he twisted the key. Muttering indecipherably, he swayed out of the wheelhouse and tripped over me in the dark groping to find a flashlight with which to inspect the recalcitrant engine. No flashlight could be located, so the only other passenger, a drunk West Villager, lit matches and held them up to the steaming motor. The wind was freshening. The boat pitched aimlessly in the fitful dark, battered by the big waves, drifting who knows where, what rocks or reefs ahead. My terror was compounded by the frustration of our having used poor judgment, having let eagerness to get home prompt us to take a risk, traveling with untrustworthy, drunk fishermen.

Without great alarm, Martin tried the engine again and again. Then, after twenty minutes, he proclaimed, "Shur, we'll row her in." Row a lobster boat? One oar was produced from below deck and the drunk passenger held it over the side of the boat faithlessly. "Pat'll see us driftin' and pick us up," he said for my sake. My eyes strained to pick out Pat's lights in the cavernous dark, but nothing was visible, land and water a churning blank. We rocked and tumbled. It was almost weirdly pleasant, drifting blindly out there. Then I noticed that Martin had turned out our lights.

We were a blank too—he wouldn't let his pride be
dented by our being seen drifting; so we wouldn't be
found, they were resigned. We were lost at sea, a half-
hour off course, moving southwest toward a litter of
tiny islands, at the mercy of the northeast wind. The
boat would break up. I was the only swimmer. How
many minutes could one survive in the frigid sea?
Owen, like the islanders, had gone passive; he was ready
to die. I clutched at him, incredulous and suddenly
furious. What was wrong with them all? Why were they
being drawn into the dark without a fight? Why hadn't
Owen learned to swim? Why wasn't he saying anything,
sitting there waiting as if a voice would come to direct
him again as it had in Aran? I could no longer contain
myself and erupted at Martin—Send up a signal, Put the
lights back on, Where's your brother, Why not drop
anchor, Do *something!* Owen tried to hush me, embarrassed and too much a willing partner in the quiet
communal drift toward death. Martin turned, confused, and chose only one of my questions to answer:
"Where's me brother? Ye heard tell of boats that pass
in the night? Well, some see ye, and some don't." So it
was all in the realm of poetry and family melodrama:
we were to be victims of grudge and pride, childish
treachery, the characters in a story that would be told
in the pub for generations to come—there was that consolation anyway.

"We'll give 'er one more try"—Martin roused
himself. And this time, in the maddening, inexplicable
way of engines, the motor caught and roared and the
craft had power again.

But it had no direction. Martin could only guess
where we had ended up, and slowly chugged into the
wind, assuming it still northeast, trying to find some
light, some clue to our whereabouts. We journeyed

blindly for what seemed hours and I still looked optimistically for Pat's lights, for boats I was sure must be out searching for us; but there was just the undifferentiated dark. At last the men picked out the harbor lighthouse, the battery-charged beacon beyond the castle, and slipped gingerly between it and Bishop's Rock into the harbor. At the mooring, Pat's boat rocked smugly, long empty, and no one was waiting concerned on the quay. Mingled with my joy at footfall on land was fury at such foolish risks and the lack of necessary camaraderie among boatmen—that family rifts could allow such callous disregard, such dangerous indifference, knowing that a boat carrying four people had left ten minutes before him and wasn't in. Here was the island's wicked potential, the depths of vindictiveness they would stoop to. I collapsed shivering into bed, holding down my rising hysteria, while Owen talked about how lucky we were.

Next morning I saw Jack on the quay sniffing the wind. "Did you hear of our great adventure, Jack?" I asked him. Of course he'd heard. The whole island had heard. "Ye were lucky itself," he glowered at me—almost as if to say we'd deserved the worst, having been stupid enough to sail with anyone but him. "Shur those old lobster boats are worthless. How can ye travel in a boat that has no mast on it so as when the engine dies on ye ye have no way to run 'er? And no way to row 'er either. It's a poor job entirely, that class of boat."

I muttered my agreement as we stood watching the spray at the tip of the harbor veil the castle in lacy outbursts. Jack wasn't going out today either. His squared shoulders met the wind and his squinting eyes met it. "Aye, there use'd be iron men on wooden ships," he chewed in summary, "and now there's only wooden men on iron ships. That's the way now."

The island is stunned. A young island girl has died in a motorcycle accident on the mainland. Half the island has never even seen a motorcycle and doesn't understand, just mutters, "A tragedy," "God's will." Deirdre was a sixteen-year-old beauty, a red-headed hoyden rushing at life. And she was Sean's adored niece (he has one married sister on the island). He is inconsolable, especially so soon after Michael Hammers's death. He repeats the wrenching details of Deirdre's accident over and over as he sobs—the curve on the Galway road we've often remarked upon, the telephone pole they hit, the boy only scratched but Deirdre's head smashed, how the priest walked out to his brother-in-law in a field to tell him, how the funeral home pinned black crepe around her face so they wouldn't see the head, not a thing else wrong with her, just her head, and she was gone.

I could see her falling. I remember so vividly a trip in on the boat with her last autumn, a wild windy day when the children were coming home from boarding school for their Halloween break. The boat tossed and slammed. Jack pushed the rudder with his whole body, leaning into the waves. We huddled on deck beneath a tarpaulin, intimate and giggly with teenagers who were giddy for home. Deirdre was their leader, their loud and daring one in blue jeans and a bright red jacket. When a violent wave smashed the boat and turned the deck nearly perpendicular to the sea, and we all started sliding off, we screamed and grabbed ropes and planks and each other, but Deirdre held on to nothing, slid straight into the rail of the boat while we gasped at her, our arms impotently reaching to save her. She let herself fly, I can still see it, right for the sea. I don't want to believe her flight has been broken, that she's hit ground.

The frightened make judgment on her—"She was a wild girl altogether. Why else would she be ridin' on one of them motorcycles with a boy?" The island's been struck at by something it doesn't understand, a spirit and a vehicle not native to it. The outer world has snatched one of its darlings, just as ruthlessly as the fairies always picked the prettiest ones to steal away to the liss. Pretty, spirited, irreverent Deirdre has been taken to the graveyard by an uncomprehending crowd.

Gloom has set in and it's twisted itself into bitterness, the physical and emotional abuse of the season breeding outburst. We've run into severe fuel shortages—gas drums are fought over on the quay. Clochan is at the end of the delivery line, and we are an end past the end. The deliveries are few and meager, and people are suffering. Like others, we've been forced to forgo our gas heater in order to save enough gas to cook with. The school is virtually heatless, the turf fire doing little good in that big, draughty room, and a group of parents have decided to call a strike and keep their children home until the heating and other problems are corrected. An uncharacteristic boldness and decisiveness in this has taken the island by surprise. Maybe it was the success of the "second line" uproar—we now have a radio telephone line to back up the cable, and it came just in time as the cable's gone out repeatedly during the last month's violent storms. Activism worked in that instance so now the island's turned its pent-up energies toward another goal—pressuring the government to put in running water. This is a major issue at the school along with the lack of heat because the children are still using a latrine. Some mothers insist that's the cause of their illnesses (though most of their facilities at home aren't any better) and have now widened the revolt to include Catherine—an attack on the casualness of the medical care. One act of protest has unleashed every complaint on the island. All anyone talks about when they meet on the road are these various "campaigns," the energy of which grittily battles against the winter—no hibernation this year. Catherine's shocked at the ferocity of the complaints, says it's unprecedented, and is in quiet negotiation with the priest and her mainland supervisors. She will probably establish official hours of business at the clinic, a couple of hours every morning, to appease those who don't enjoy doing business in her kitchen. Set hours will provide some sense of entitlement and privacy, which, of course, will be a great improvement.

The anger that's been whipped up around these issues is shocking though. Unfortunately, Harold is behind a lot of it, stirring up battened-down wills with jargon and his own frustrations. He is feeding off the reality of the appalling conditions of the islanders' lives, revolutionizing, but feeding as well off their childish wickedness, their appetite to do one another in. They are using him as catalyst, rallying point, mouthpiece. Now he has a spiteful project in the works: a co-op that would bring in farm goods and groceries in bulk to sell wholesale—a direct attack, in other words, on Bridget and Richard, the two shopowners. A small band of West Village malcontents is in this with him—they're the ones with no shop of their own who must spend all their money to the East. The purpose seems principally, though, to deny the money to Richard and Catherine who've been turned into the wealthy against whom the poor can vent their frustration. In this case, one family is not only the entire upper class, but also the controllers of medical care, food, fuel, and tourism.

We are in a curious position, suspect to some and anathema to Harold, because of our closeness to Catherine. Conversation with neighbors sometimes freezes when I casually mention her. The demarcations of class are clear, and we have been thrust, unwillingly, and unbeknownst to ourselves, on the side of the establishment. The notion is ludicrous—we are equally close to Sean and others. But we've no intention of abandoning Catherine now that she's suddenly the target of revolt.

And I am ambivalent about what role we ought to play in any case. I didn't come here to try to change island life, I came to change my own life, and as an outsider, I've always felt I should stand back from their quarrels. Though I naturally wish the islanders health and comfort, I'm sickened by the hatred and suffering their transitions to modern life are provoking. These are the things I came to the island to avoid, and now I'm faced with having to choose sides in a battle neither side of which I'm wholehearted about.

The winter has bred a plethora of committees: water committee, medical committee, school committee, co-op committee, general development committee. The gaslight burns late into the night in the cold schoolhouse, though it's empty all day, and the tension grows daily. No one has stepped forward to call a halt, make the peace. The idealistic priest is overwhelmed and depressed, unable to restore order. First and foremost he wants the children back in school, but can only promise his good intentions to use his influence to get improvements. The parents won't budge, an obstreperousness no one would have predicted. This new breed of priest has been easy for them to defy, so they're taking ad-

vantage of their sudden power. Anger seldom expressed
has billowed the sails of more anger. We're being blown
along an uncharted route in an unwieldy craft.

Until recently, I didn't realize the depth of this
dark side of the island. It is well hidden behind the
regularity of habits and the island's chattering public
face. It's easy to overlook that some never speak, easy
not to imagine the worst of whispered conversations
behind stone walls, easy to forget that half the population has essentially no public life—women locked into
their exhausting routines with no communal outlet.
Easy not to have seen the potential for warfare. It was
easy because I was enchanted by the surface of it all—its
beauty, oddity, talkativeness.

I've luxuriated in the island mist for nearly five
years. Just as in the legend, perhaps a spark of fire from
the outer world could suddenly solidify me, lift me out
of the charmed fog. What kind of fire? This political
upheaval, the stimulation of our time in Dublin, time
away from Owen? Do I really want to be disenchanted,
to see myself, my island, in the clear, hard, non-Atlantic
light?

The caravan for Mary and Gerald came in on a night
of sudden calm but thick fog. It had been waiting a
week on Clochan quay, so Jack decided to risk it, strapping it crossways over the deck so it hung off each side.
It completely blocked Jack's view, so Jamesy was sent
to perch atop it as navigator. But there was little to
navigate from as night fell and not a light could be
gleaned. Twice they lost their way and found themselves by the island's eastern rocky shore. A crowd

gathered anxiously on the quay, fearing the worst by reflex. Fog tented us, accentuating the smell of turf smoke, dung, and the nervous men. When the boat eventually inched around the tower, a huge misshapen apparition with a man on top emerging from mist, the quay was fidgety with the release of tension and curiosity about the cargo. The boat skimmed up the harbor to the quay where the tide was now dropping fast, and twenty men leapt on board to help untie the caravan, put planks in place, and roll her off. There she was, a mobile home, right in the middle of the quay amidst lobster pots and rotting boats and empty gas drums. Gerald took a key ceremoniously from his pocket, opened the door and tiptoed in with Mary while the crowd waited outside on tenterhooks. Finally Mary gave the signal, "Come on," and the women pushed to get in to inspect it, jamming the narrow aisle, opening and closing every cubbyhole cabinet it had, unfolding and trying the beds, a nosey housewarming, prejudice overwhelmed by novelty, Mary and Gerald, now safely wed and the possessors of a caravan, feted at last. Today a tractor towed the new island home to its permanent location where it was tied down to stakes to keep it grounded.

The specter of Sean haunts the winter. He is a broken man since the deaths of Michael Hammers and Deirdre and cannot be nudged back to life. He wanders on the strand all day picking winkles though there's little money to make on them. He does it to be alone. At night he drinks in the corner of the pub, away from company, his face to the floor. When we try to talk to him, he begins to cry and says, "I'm finished, I'm finished." "That's the winter talking," Owen says, but Sean shakes his head no. The loss of Deirdre is as great as the loss of a daughter to him—the only girl-child he ever had to love, the only girl he loved since he lost the one who left. And all his losses have now become the loss of Deirdre—all the more poignant because of the kind of girl she was, because she had all the energy and gaiety Sean himself once had.

Everything's conspiring to add to Sean's gloom. This is the worst winter we've had yet, unrelieved gales and a deep freeze, the boat cowering at its mooring week after week. The gas shortage is so severe now—a national crisis—that we're down to one dwindling drum. I've stopped washing clothes, waiting for relief, and do all the cooking in one shot each day, cramming the oven with bread, casseroles, and potatoes. Even after the flurry of Dublin work, we've barely enough money— just enough to get through to Owen's next series of radio scripts in the spring. True to Harold's unhappy predictions, the cost of living has gone over the top since Ireland joined the Common Market and it's no longer possible to live here as we did at first. The islanders' situation has improved slightly, but nothing's improved for us. The dribs and drabs of free-lance work we do pay the same preinflation fees and don't provide enough for even minimal necessities, so we're falling back instead of inching forward, reducing our needs and desires.

It has an edge of madness. Lack of light, heat, and good food rob me of emotional stamina. I fear getting sick, being stranded, losing my balance. I wait for something to break, for something to happen. I imagine it will come in the mail—word, opportunity, an alternative that can't be denied. I wait for the storms to break only so the mail will come.

The Last Winter

The islanders bow down under the weather, the misery demeaning, unfathomable. So much of their character is clearer to me now, sharing this winter with them: their harbored grudges and bitterness, hard self-hatred and manic summer energy—their bodies and psyches acclimated to this harsh inevitable cycle. Their stubborn clinging to habits and proprieties saves them, perhaps, but also does them in. Where is the psychic nourishment that can rescue Sean from his despair? No one can provide it, with their reticence or indifference or whatever it is that keeps them from expressing anything but a casual talkative concern, keeping a social even keel. Where is the common sense that can nourish Eileen's children and keep them out of the clinic with flus? They get almost no protein, subsist on potatoes and scones and jam and cake. With the cows close to calfing there's not even the usual milk, and Eileen's too proud to eat salted fish. She rails against the world for their sickliness and rotting teeth. Pregnant with another child, she eats just as poorly herself. Is it impossible for her to be educated, to buy tinned meat or cheese instead of jam, go back to salted fish and shellfish even? If things were better Eileen would lose the righteousness of complaint on which she and the others have come to depend. The only changes they'll accept are conveniences, things to make chores simpler.

In my pessimism over the impotence of someone like Eileen, I can't help but side with Catherine and her indomitable will, even if it is ruthless or self-serving at times. She at least shapes her existence instead of succumbing to it. And that has been just as much a part of the island's natural character as the passivity of colonialism has been.

On a special run of the boat at five, three men from the County Council came in all the way from Galway, in response to the recent turmoil, to hold a public hearing on the future needs of the island. They are spending the night at the hotel. Eileen scowls, "Shur, what'll they learn about the island stayin' there? It's in a house with no water they should stick 'em."

At seven the priest opens the hall. It is the climax of the winter's campaigns. Harold has been preparing all week, rehearsing his hand-picked islanders with the speeches he really wants to make himself but must, in the circumstances, have come from their mouths. The speechmakers have bathed midweek and put on their Sunday suits—a first for a secular occasion. Unprotected by their usual layers of grime, they are vulnerable, shy. It's easy to commit oneself to points of view over a pint in the corner of the pub, but to stand up publicly before the congregation of the island and denounce or demand is an unfamiliar task.

Catherine looks solemn but self-possessed, while Harold beadily eyes the crowd, already tasting the blood that will be spilled. The priest nervously convenes the meeting and introduces the County Council members. One of them addresses us, says they've come to listen, there are no funds at the moment, they can make no promises tonight . . . but they want to hear what we have to say. Owen and I sit quietly at the rear.

A West Villager rises and airs a wan plea for running water: "It's the water we're wantin'. It's a hard thing not havin' the water. The cows, ye know, and the little children, the poor divils. Wouldn't it be a grand thing now to have a tap at the house?" He sits down. The councilmen nod sagely. Maura, our veteran car owner, unexpectedly rises to make a plea for paved roads. The crowd glares at her. "Let her fall in a ditch in her damned car," Bridget mutters within our earshot. Then the more passionate speeches: heat in the school, the medical service, electricity. The pitch rises. People steal glances at Catherine to see her response, but she's impassive. She's already had her word with the county councilmen over dinner. They're well fed, sleepy. Nothing much will come of this meeting.

Harold rises for a finale: "It should be clear to you from what you've heard tonight that this island struggles under systematic deprivation. This is not a matter of benign neglect, but willful deprivation due to a system that supports greed and selfishness and the perpetuation of a class division—" he's gone schoolmasterly; the councilmen fidget and the islanders stare in awe, uncomprehending. And then: "No need to mention names, but there are people on this island who will do anything to keep their advantage, and others who will connive with them so that power won't be yielded and substantive changes never made, which is a pastime of the most insidious sort. You should be quite clear what the voice of the island is saying when you review your applications for grants for hotel expansions—it is the voice you've heard in this room tonight demanding heat, water, medical care." He sits down and the room holds its breath, but the roof doesn't fall in.

The priest rises to break the anxious spell and says awkwardly, "I'm sure the Council representatives have appreciated what everyone had to say and appreciate your coming out on a bad night like this to welcome them. Good night and God bless." The crowd stirs to exit. Harold walks right up to Catherine and says in a loud voice, "Now you know where to stuff your fucking hotel." The priest and councilmen blanch. Owen bolts up to intervene—the suggestion that the hotel in any way competes with funds for basic improvements is slanderous—but Harold raises his hands in mock surrender, smiles, and leaves. Sean says to a trembling Catherine, "Shur, never mind that madman." A councilman jokes, "That's why we have two ears—for it to

218

go in one and out the other." Another says, "That man sure has a chip on his shoulder," and Sean shoots back, "Shur, he has a whole forest growin' on his back." There's consolation, anyway, in having Sean's sense of humor roused again.

We walk out shaken. I'm not happy to be walking out with the county councilmen, the priest, and Catherine, to have somehow ended up on their side through my friendship with her. The entire evening will probably go in one ear of the County Council and out the other. The islanders will be left even more frustrated and angry. They are learning how to fight battles and shape their own lives, though, and that can't but be good for them. They won't go down without a fight like The Great Blasket and Gentle Island did—perhaps they'll rage and win. Maybe they've learned something from those experiences, or from television, or tourists. Maybe no more islands will let themselves die. But Catherine is not the villain, no fat cat they must crucify in order to make progress—she's come out of terrible poverty and powerlessness herself, and though she clings to what she's gained, her native goodness prevails.

She's been badly hurt by the island's evident resentment of her. As we leave for home, she says bittersweetly that she'll come up tomorrow afternoon for a "postmortem" on the meeting. Sean, drifting jauntily toward the pub, shouts back, "Ye'd really want to be a pathologist, Catherine."

That is the last thing we ever heard Sean say. The next morning The Flame rapped at our kitchen window, his

cap low over his face, and said, "Yur needed, Owen"—
the summons of emergencies.

"What is it?" We walked out.

"Sean is missin'." Missing? How could a person
be missing on an island?

"What do you mean, missing?"

"The villages is searched so now we're goin' out.
Yur curragh is wanted."

The import began to crawl up my body.

Owen put on his oilskins in a daze and headed
for our boat. It was ashore for the winter, but five men
hoisted it atop their heads and walked it down to the
water, ten legs topped by a wet carapace. I stood on
shore with Catherine. "I'd say he just walked into the
sea," she wept. How could she know? Had they stood
like this before, someone inexplicably vanished, and
reached the only conclusion possible? I couldn't yield
to it. "He must have fallen on the way home, maybe
broken an arm or leg. He could be lying in a ditch or a
barn." I forgot that The Flame said the villages had
already been searched. Catherine put her arm around
me and said he'd never been the same since Deirdre
died.

We walked to Rosie's to join the vigil of women
waiting while the men searched. Rosie already knew,
as I refused to, and was mourning, softly rocking her
head forward and back, weeping. "His dog was barkin'
at the door, and there was no sign of 'im," she repeated
as each newcomer came up to comfort her. Ann glared,
angry at the fuss, at the shameful exposure.

Oh God, what had we missed, what hadn't we
seen or said? The night of the meeting he'd seemed
himself again for the first time since Deirdre's death.
But had we listened closely enough, ever?—the night he
told us how he'd lost the girl he loved, the nights he
longed miserably for summer, the night he said he was

"finished." Had we or anyone tried hard enough to convince him that he wasn't?

"His memory was gone," a woman says, a village elder, presiding—a euphemism for his sanity, his control. But it's ironic: it was his memory that was most present, that always overshadowed the future, his inability to forget, to give up his ghosts. The sparkle of his personality was his compulsion to remember, but remembering too much was also his doom.

Nothing happened that day or the next. The sea stubbornly refused to give us back its prize. Sean was still "missing," and life went on in an unbearable limbo. The Flame said it would take a week, that bodies don't rise from the sea floor till the brain rots. "Ye think the body is heavy?" he says. "It's as light as a feather. It's the brain that keeps 'em down. Yes sir, it's the brain that's heavy." A storm came and the search was called off. Every man in the pub reminisced, recalled the last time he had seen Sean, but no one had an illumination, just empty pub-talk theorizing. On the seventh day, when the storm fell away, Sean's body was seen floating off the northeast corner of the island, near the end of "The Hag's Causeway."

Because it was an "accidental" death, an official inquest was required by the county, which had gotten wind of the search. Three men in a curragh rowed Sean's poor waterlogged body around to the East Village bay and Jack sailed around to meet it there and take it out to the mainland. We gathered on the quay at a horrified distance as the priest met the corpse. At least there was going to be no talk of suicide, no denial of rites.

No one could say Sean hadn't fallen into the sea. No, no one could say that—it could be he was drunk, or under a hag's spell cast on those red stones, or that a breath of wind took him. Or that he was just

thinking by the edge of the sea—what was he thinking?—
and lost his balance. The way the whole island has lost
its balance. "This is the worst year for tragedies, ever,"
Bridget sobbed beside me. Was that really Sean down
there in a bundle of green canvas? I couldn't breathe,
so great was my disbelief and pain. Bridget was shaking
her head. The island was wrung out, there were no
more resources for this new grief.

Sean's body came in from the mainland on a moonless,
churlish night. At the harbor, the tide ebbed and there
was one crying guillemot to be heard. Behind walls, lit
pipes and cigarettes bobbed in conversation. Sean had
gone out in a green tarpaulin, but returned in a polished coffin, Ann a huddled guardian on deck. We
began again that hauntingly familiar routine—the short
walk with the coffin to the church, a few prayers, then
next morning the mass, the procession to the graveyard,
this time in splashing rain, the mud, the stones laid on
top of the filled-in earth, the handfuls of sodden flowers.
And it was over. We were back in the bar where Sean
will never again joke nor laugh as if his body would
break, where Tommy will never again malign or fanta-
size. Richard's pub, the vital cacophonous center, is a
quieter, less comradely center than in our early days
here, its centering personalities gone.

A surly sadness reigns instead. Less likelihood
of relieving pain in cadenzas of wit. More likely that an
argument will be picked. Or a sullen silence. Was such
angry defeat always in this room, only less overt, dif-
fused by the likes of Sean? Was it always clear, but were
my eyes clouded to it? Or has it really happened that

misery has mounted year after year, that we're in a
pressure cooker of discontent that was bound to blow its
top? Perhaps one dark night, unbeknownst to us, that
white cow climbed out of the lake, surveyed us with
disappointment, and slipped back in, bringing in the
wake of her gaze "the worst year for tragedies," the
seven-year round of despair. Before long maybe her influence will fade and six more charmed years be ours.
Maybe.

We'd always thought it was Tommy, not Sean,
who would come to a bad end, poisoned as he was. But
maybe his vociferousness saved him—his crying out the
sign that he wanted to be rescued. It's no ideal life he's
been plunked down into, six days a week in a clothing
factory, with a wife and two young children now in a
three-room flat, but it's a life that allows some outlet
for his affections and energy. When he comes home to
visit, though, he gloats in his separateness, his "English-
ness" by association, takes pains to prove how hard it
is for him to be home on the island again. So the solution has its great price—a man severed from his home
culture, and a culture denuded of its most talented
members. It's hard to see how someone like Tommy
could have stayed here and thrived. Given his intelligence, how could he not lust for travel, contact, experience? As an outsider, I longed for the island to accommodate him, make it possible for him to stay, to know
that the likes of Tommy are its real hope, the energy
of the young who have a balanced view of the outer
world but choose to return, choose to shape the island's
future with the best of their tradition and the best of
their education and experience. A naive ideal, perhaps,
but there is hope in people like Gerald and Mary.

And Sean, who always seemed to me to have the
great talent of survival with grace, was the one who
couldn't make it. His suicide has ripped through the

island like a knife—his lifetime of coping and kindness blasted by his final gesture of defeat. We should have seen—he should have wept and railed more.

Sean's death has robbed us of one of our deepest connections to the island. He and the best of the island were fused in our minds from the start. His disappearance feels like the climax to our story; being here without him feels like being in someone else's story instead of our own.

Without forethought or plans, I've found myself sorting through papers and clothes the last few days, packing away, throwing out, lightening our load, as if I knew we were leaving, as if I knew where we were going or when. Owen watches, pained. I don't know where I want to go or how, just that I'm bereft, ready.

This morning I thought I'd go out on a quick shopping trip to Clifden. I stood on the quay trying to get Jack to commit himself to wait for me in Clochan for an hour so I could get back in right away on the boat. He said he wouldn't be "delayin'," but as usual, he refused to be more specific. I urged, "But I have to be sure I can get back in—I don't want to stay out the night." Finally, he obliquely obliged by saying, "Ye can't come in if ye don't go out, so ye might as well go out." So I do.

But as soon as we leave the harbor, I begin to cry. Jack sits down beside me, says nothing. As I watch the island narrow and fade behind us, I have a terrible dread that I will never see it again, that I will die today on the mainland. But I know my fear must mean that I've given up the island in my heart. Watching it vanish, that inevitability seems unbearable.

There afloat in the channel, the great divide of our lives, I know that this gaunt and gorgeous island has incongruously become a womb, an evasion instead of an outpost. But perhaps, in the end, the island was no escape from reality at all, just a different reality with its own abominations and terrible death throes, and I'm as unprepared to deal with pain here as elsewhere. Staying, I might in time become as bitter as Harold. Leaving, I confront unknown perils. I fell in love with a dying culture and now must cut myself free of it before it drags me down with it. I will be one of the quitters, like the emigrants, tourists, and Sean, but I mean to save my life.

Jack stares into the sea, measuring the alignment of rocks that signals the halfway point to Clochan. Jack, a mystic of the seascape, spends his life going back and forth, day in, day out. I would like that fluidity—to go out, do something to make me feel adept in the world again, allow me a career, but to come back, amphibious. It's the last thing Owen wants to do. He spent too many frustrating years out there already. But I rejected the world too soon, retired in advance of having lived. He says it's unfair to drag him back and to expect his help for reentry. But though it takes all my will power to make a decision that will cause him pain, I remember well how he defended his choice of five years ago, leaving his family and bringing us here— "There's no fairness in the world." It is my turn, I think, to be unfair.

The boat pulls into Clochan. We tie up and Jack walks me up the long quay. Now he says kindly, "Take yur time"—he'll wait for me long as necessary. I hire a car to Clifden, buy a newspaper and a good hot lunch to linger over, knowing he'll be there when I'm ready to go back in.

Epilogue

We must go with the world even when it takes the wrong path, but the old way was the better.

—A Blasket Islander

On the Island of the White Cow there are 190 people left. When I meet them, they cock their heads and cry, "How's Deba?" though it's five years since I met them last on these (still unpaved) roads. For each questioner I must provide every detail of the last five years of my life. In return, they tell me the island's.

There have been twenty-three deaths and eleven departures, but only six births in these past five years. The newly married women are "spacing" their babies, but no one's asking too many questions about how. "A dying island" is the phrase on the lips of most—the perennial pessimists. "Nothing's changed since ye's left," an old man tells me. Not true—plenty has changed.

That last season's strife has reaped its rewards—running water's been installed, the schoolhouse has been renovated and provided with two large gas heaters, and Catherine opens the clinic for two hours every morning but Sunday to see patients. Progress. Once the battles were won, life settled back to normal. The houses look a little more chipper, the hotel's added a wing—the islanders look as if they're here to stay. Still, they complain and despair of the future as they modernize their kitchens.

I walk down to the well my first morning back, not to draw water—I'm staying in the hotel with Catherine—but as a ritual gesture of return. I lift the big rock lid that's kept on the well to prevent the cows that wander along the shore from drinking out of it, and beneath the lid I find a thick spider web completely covering the well's mouth. It's unused now. Piped chlorinated water's replaced the spring, water so heavily chlorinated that people have to throw out their kettles yearly. They say young Pat Hehir, in charge of dumping the stuff into the system, gets the measurements all wrong, especially when he "has a few drinks taken." They don't consider what that might mean for their bodies. They've thrown out their buckets.

In the States, every Saturday morning I get in my car and drive ten miles to a spring to fill one-gallon plastic containers with fresh spring water for the week. Stowing them in the trunk, I always think of the island, feel as if I've been to the well. It's a compensation. For there is little else to remind me of the island in the life I've chosen, a life full of the compromises and difficulties I knew it would have.

When we left the island, it was supposed to be temporary, for the academic year. I'd enrolled in graduate school and Owen had gotten a visiting appointment at a nearby college out of support for me, for he hated the thought of teaching again. We planned to be back on the island for the summer. Catherine stood at the end of the quay crying and waving until her arm looked like a piece of flotsam in the breeze. And then it fell away and we were gone, free. Catrina said that when we got on line at the airport in Dublin with a crowd of American tourists, I was instantly reabsorbed, unexiled before her eyes. She was sure the return would be good for me.

But after three months everything fell apart. Nothing in our island life with its regularity and dramatic hardships had prepared us for a life of conflicting schedules, dull chores, and adjustment to the urban. I was shakily back in home territory, testing my old voice; Owen was back in what was for him a horror, and rapidly grew resentful. By the end of the school year we'd separated. Owen went to Dublin; I went to New York to find a job. Catherine cleared out the house, surprised to find everything neatly packed in boxes. She mailed the books and souvenirs I asked for and stored the rest at her place. Owen wanted no reminders.

In Clochan, Jack gave me a hug, said, "Where's yur gear?" as if I were coming in from a mere shopping jaunt, dropped my bag in the hold, and got back to work. He and Jamesy and Jack's son, now being groomed as future skipper ("Things'll never be the same," the islanders complain, "all this young crowd drinks"), were getting the pulley ready on the mast to load the deck. Jack pointed to a pile of long greasy poles behind me. "Do ye know what those are?" I turned and stared. "Electricity! They're puttin' in the electricity." So they'd finally reached that glorious moment, that goal too elusive to even fight for in the winter of their discontent five years ago. The poles were bound, lifted, and then floated through the air, docile. The deck was quickly covered and I had to climb over poles to find a place to sit on the hatch.

I was sailing in with the first signs of a new era, just as I was entering a new era myself in the States—my first teaching job. I held the island and myself up against each other to measure our progress. "It's a dying island," Jack said, though all these improvements are

231

visible and boasted of. "After this priest, I'd say there'll never be a priest on the island again," Jack said. "There's a shortage of priests in the diocese, ye know, and the islands'll be the first to lose 'em. And when there's no priest anymores, none of the young people will stay." There's never been a priest on Boar, but the White Cow always prided itself as a deserving spot.

There's a new priest here now though. The priest who was interested in Zen succumbed to the treachery of island politics and fled, battered. He wrote to us in the States: "You must have been torn, as I was, leaving. The island holds such a terrible fascination for those of us who haven't been reared to it, but there's an element of fantasy to its hold on one, don't you think?" There seems little of the fantastic around me at the moment. A conservative, experienced priest was sent in to replace our friend and order was quickly restored.

Harold has left, gone to another island up the coast to start over again—a new audience, new ground to break. With his and our departures, there are no nonislanders here now except in the summer when the influx is greater than ever.

Theresa's brother died last spring in Pittsburgh, never having returned to live on the island as he'd promised. Bridget's husband died two years ago and everyone waited for her to catch the next plane to New York as she'd been dreaming out loud of doing for years. But she didn't. She's still here, complaining how much better things are in the States, but unable, after all, to leave home.

Tommy has three children, is assistant manager at his factory, and is living in a square prefab house outside of London. He comes home each year for a week, in August.

Rosie's now close to ninety and bursts into tears as I walk in the door. "Well would ye recognize this place a'tall as the same place as when ye's came first? The old folks gone and the young crowd, they don't have the *nature* in 'em, not a bit of it. My heart is broke sittin' here since Sean was lost. Broke entirely."

The most avaricious man on the island, always looking to make a few pence off a tourist, stops me on the road, doesn't recognize me. "How're ye enjoyin' yur holidays?"

"Very well, thank you."

We chat about the weather, the view. "Isn't that a grand garden there?" He points to his own garden.

"It is indeed," I agree, suppressing my knowing laughter.

"Well, that's my garden, so if yur needin' any vegetables durin' yur holidays, ye know where to ask."

"Thanks very much." I don't let on.

I wonder, were I a stranger, would I think him charming and helpful, rather than ingratiating and opportunistic?

Almost every household has a television running off a car battery. By Christmas they can switch to a plug in the wall. I go to call on Gerald and Mary in their now rusty, delapidated caravan which despite its other deprivations is topped with an antenna. Always when I called in the past I was warmly greeted with tea and scones. Tonight we hug, then settle down to a game show, Gerald and Mary and their three children, hypnotized by the tube instead of the fire. We hardly speak. But they want to know what's going to happen on *Dallas*—the Irish season is a couple of months behind ours. I haven't watched *Dallas* so can't help them. They're surprised, thought all Americans watch *Dallas*.

Epilogue

After an hour and a half of TV, I leave, knowing little of what's happened to them the past five years, but perhaps needing no explanations.

I've come back because I had to, and to see if there's some way to capture all my tenderness for this place in writing. Guiltily, I find myself asking Catherine to retell a story, or get Richard to explain the derivation of a name. They don't know my intention. While I was here I respected a self-imposed prohibition against writing about the island, wrote only a handful of innocent poems, proved I was here because I truly loved the island by not using it as material. But I have decided I must document this place, must take up the record lost with Joe Coyne and Sean and Tommy because I fear no one here is taking it up, and I can't bear the thought of its loss.

For a short time I was privy to a vanishing world, a last fringe, a fragile land that any time now might be repossessed, returned to mist and seaweed. What can I say to say good-bye? I'm unable to reach conclusions. I say: here is my island, its colors, its voices, its losses. This, a long letter home.

From 1972 to 1977, DEBORAH TALL lived on the Irish island described in this book, growing vegetables, writing poetry, and doing freelance work for *The Irish Press* and Radio Telefis Eireann. On her return to the U.S., she received an M.F.A. from Goddard College and has been teaching since, currently at Hobart and William Smith Colleges in Geneva, New York, where she edits the *Seneca Review*. She won the Hopwood Award for Poetry while studying for her B.A. at the University of Michigan, and her poetry has been published widely; her most recent collection is *Ninth Life* from Ithaca House. She's also the author of a libretto for an operatic adaptation of the early Irish epic *The Tain* entitled *The Cattle Raid on Cooley*. Ms. Tall lives in upstate New York with her husband, David Weiss, and daughter, Zoe.